Praise for *Burnout Recovery*

"One of the most insightful and compassionate guides for those navigating the complex terrain of burnout. Using a vivid and accessible wildfire metaphor, Alicia gently walks readers through the stages of collapse and recovery. Her book offers practical tools, personal stories, and reflective guidance for understanding where you are in the burnout cycle and how to begin again. Whether you're dealing with workplace exhaustion, neurodivergent burnout, or chronic illness, or seeking ways to prevent future flare-ups, this book provides a healing road map that is both deeply validating and profoundly useful."

—EMELY RUMBLE, LCSW, author of *Bibliotherapy in the Bronx*

"This powerful and compassionate book approaches burnout not as a single event but as an all-encompassing experience that can touch every layer of our lives: professionally, personally, and even in how we see ourselves. . . . The sections addressing neurodivergent experiences, the mental load at home, career shifts, and long-term recovery are what make this book special. This author offers a clear, hopeful road map for recognizing where you are in the cycle, finding relief, and cultivating a healthier, more sustainable way forward if you're coping with burnout."

—LAURA BRIGGS, author of *The Six-Figure Freelancer*

"This book sparks breakthrough after breakthrough for anyone who's tried everything and still feels stuck. It's a lifeline for sensitive, creative minds; the reset button your soul has been waiting for; one of those rare guides that shows you what's really happening and how to break free. This book makes burnout recovery feel possible, even beautiful."

—MARY CANNON, trademark lawyer for entrepreneurs and creatives

"Alicia K. Anderson has crafted something refreshingly different by viewing the concept of burnout through the powerful lens of wildfire ecology and storytelling. . . . Her expansion beyond workplace burnout to address the often-overlooked issue of neurodivergent burnout is particularly valuable. Her personal experience with autism and chronic illness brings authenticity and nuance to discussions that are often only surface level in other books.

One of the book's greatest strengths lies in its actionable approach. Rather than simply diagnosing the problem, *Burnout Recovery* provides concrete exercises, rituals, and support strategies that acknowledge burnout as a systemic issue while empowering individual healing. This is essential reading for anyone seeking to heal from burnout or support others through it."

—FIONA WILKINSON, PsyD, behavioral psychologist, psychological
    therapist, and ADHD clinician

"Alicia beautifully explores the metaphor of a wildfire and flood to guide people in unpacking their burnout and grief. The exercises throughout the book allow us to deeply reflect on our work and family lives, create boundaries, and empower us to find a way forward through the wildfire to restoration. Her metaphors and vulnerability give us permission to be equally vulnerable as we process our burnout."

—JESSICA SHANNON, MDiv, BCC

"Dr. Anderson's extraordinary work, applying ecopsychology and natural world cycles to the 'feature' of burnout that current generations experience, reintroduces ancient, deep, biological life cycle wisdom to an AI-driven world. Stressors abound in our overstimulated evirons. Alicia's work is a significant contribution to managing the undergrowth and minimizing runaway wildfire while enabling recovery and nurturing new life from the ashfall."

—NATHAN HOGAN, PhD, vice president of One Tree Learning Institute

"This book is one of the most powerful that I have read to help clients who are at a crossroads in their careers. Based in science, written with deep understanding, and full of practical exercises to help clients gain clarity, *Burnout Recovery* is a great resource for career and leadership coaches who work with clients to move away from burnout to build (and sustain) a satisfying career."

—JUDY BERMAN, career and leadership coach

"Alicia's timely *Burnout Recovery* offers readers a much-needed breath of fresh air and sight of the promising horizon that is typically covered by thick smoke. Her step-by-step, fireproof guidance draws from her deep knowledge and her own close encounters with wildfires, distilled in easy and relatable metaphoric analogies to help us assess, contain, and heal our own relationship to burnout. Convinced that it's never too late—even if we've felt stuck for years fighting fire after fire—she shows us how to detect instead of neglect our personal warning signals and dismantle default inner climate denial, using her rich lived experiences as an example.

Anderson offers us hopeful solutions and a clear road map that will not just heal burnout on a personal level—if we all do our part in preventing future burnout, we also have a fighting chance in deterring devastating climate catastrophes and wildfires that more often than not are the result of relentless drive, unsustainable exploitation, and overheating of ourselves and our Earth Mother in the name of productivity."

—LORAINE Y. VAN TUYL, PhD, CHT, Soul Authority transformational life coach, integrative clinical psychologist, and author of *Amazon Wisdom Keeper* and *Soul Authority*

Burn *out* Recovery

A Neurodivergent-Friendly Guide to Healing Burnout Through Nature's Wisdom

Alicia K. Anderson, PhD

Foreword by Linda Buzzell, MA, LMFT

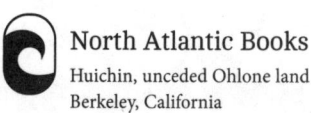

North Atlantic Books
Huichin, unceded Ohlone land
Berkeley, California

North Atlantic Books
Huichin, unceded Ohlone land
2526 Martin Luther King Jr Way
Berkeley, CA 94704 USA
www.northatlanticbooks.com

Cover art © DrPixel via Getty Images
Cover design by Jess Morphew
Book design by Happenstance Type-O-Rama

Printed in the United States of America

Burnout Recovery: A Neurodivergent-Friendly Guide to Healing Burnout Through Nature's Wisdom is sponsored and published by North Atlantic Books, an educational nonprofit that collaborates with partners to develop cross-cultural perspectives; nurture holistic views of art, science, the humanities, and healing; and seed personal and global transformation by publishing work on the relationship of body, spirit, and nature.

North Atlantic Books's publications are distributed to the US trade and internationally by Penguin Random House Publisher Services. For further information, visit our website at www.northatlanticbooks.com.

The authorized representative in the EU for product safety and compliance is Eucomply OÜ, Pärnu mnt 139b-14, 11317 Tallinn, Estonia, hello@eucompliancepartner.com, +33757690241.

Library of Congress Cataloging-in-Publication data is available from the publisher upon request.
ISBN: 979-8-88984-313-9 (paperback)
ISBN: 979-8-88984-314-6 (ebook)

1 2 3 4 5 6 7 8 9 KPC 31 30 29 28 27 26

For Kim, who leaps

Contents

Foreword

LIKE ALICIA K. ANDERSON, I live in wildfire country. I, too, am familiar with the trauma, stress, and cycles of fear connected to drought, winds, and fire. As a Californian, I now find that as each year moves into spring, visceral memories of previous years' fires, post-fire floods, and lethal mudflows begin to haunt my dreams and waking life. As I tend the fruit trees in my backyard, the joy of buds and flowers is often mixed with fears of dry days, lethal heat, smoke, evacuation, and loss. In its extreme form, this dread may be called *eco-anxiety*, a term now defined by the American Psychology Association as "a chronic fear of environmental doom."[1] In some people, it may even qualify as full-blown PTSD (post-traumatic stress disorder).

With escalating climate disruption affecting so many places around our planet, each year more and more people have intimate knowledge of and respect for the archetypal element of fire as it threatens and destroys forests, homes, and communities after long, dry seasons. Ecopsychology is the field that studies and explores these complex interrelationships between human beings and our rapidly changing natural world. The name for our field comes from three important Greek words: *oikos* (home or hearth), *psyche* (mind or soul), and *logos* (word or study). Ecopsychology, then, is the study of the relationship between the human psyche and our earthly home.

Some also conceive of ecopsychology as a marriage between the disciplines of psychology and ecology. But of course, there isn't just one form of psychology, and so there are as many different types of ecopsychology as there are schools of psychology. Additionally, there are many forms of psychological inquiry and treatment that long pre-date Sigmund Freud, including many non-Western and Indigenous ecopsychologies around the world.

As this book reveals, the field of depth psychology produces an especially resonant form of ecopsychology. Depth ecopsychology takes us well below the superficial understandings of modern life, lead-ing us into realms we often fail to fully fathom. Anderson addition-ally brings climate psychology into the mix, a form of ecopsychology which studies the mutually reinforcing effects of rapidly worsening cli-mate and ecological conditions related to the four primal elements—Fire, Air, Earth, and Water—on the human psyche. All four elements have a direct impact on wildfire—even water, whose very absence is a root cause of the dry, windy frenzies that lead to fires that destroy land, trees, and life. Anderson's skillful use of both depth ecopsychol-ogy and climate psychology allows us to explore these rapidly chang-ing relationships in new ways, providing us with useful metaphorical understandings of the complex phenomenon of wildfire and its effects on the human psyche.

With this unique mix of perspectives, Anderson helps us delve deeply into our rapidly degenerating relationship with fire and under-stand how this relates to the psychological condition of burnout. She helps us address the enormity of these challenges by exploring the relationship between the rushed, overly fiery way in which many of us now live and the growing presence of wildfire as an ecological and psy-chological reality in our lives, finding fascinating connections between the increasing threats of out-of-control wildfires and the way our cul-ture demands that we relate to work and stress. "Stress is the water we're swimming in," she tells us.

As we deal with fire as one of the four interconnected, primal ele-ments that permeate wider nature and our body-mind-soul-spirit, we also begin to see the connections between these fiery conditions of modern life and our shameful disrespect for water, healthy earth, and the powerful winds that can spread wildfire to new locations. The disruption of a balanced relationship between these primal elements brings escalating personal, community, ecological, and social/political trauma to our lives.

The metaphor of wildfire is such an apt description for psychological burnout. The very word lets us know we are touching the archetypal element of fire, with its terrifying, awe-inspiring ferocity and ability to reduce everything to ashes. It encourages us to examine our own individual and collective ways of living that involve a burning up of finite energy, a parched drought of the soul, a lack of watery fluidity, ceaseless winds of turmoil, and a disconnection from soil and earth.

Anderson also helps us understand a deeper point: that fire, when seen as part of a bigger cycle, can also offer hope. Violent destruction can bring a clearing out of underbrush, followed by the cleansing tide of watery floods and the eventual regrowth of earth's beauty and richness.

For those of us who struggle to deal in a deeper way with all these escalating challenges, this kind of deep, nature-based approach and understanding is a balm. And for those who study psychology and perhaps treat clients and patients (or ourselves and our families) for these varied, yet connected painful conditions—stress, climate trauma, burnout, eco-anxiety, grief, and terror from escalating collective threats and losses—this book offers a new and helpful perspective on the fires now raging through our world.

—*LINDA BUZZELL, MA, LMFT; founder of*
the International Association for Ecotherapy

Introduction

"BURNOUT" IS A WORD that has been used so many times that it can feel like it has lost its meaning. Since an estimated 77–89 percent of adults are now reporting feelings of burnout, it also can begin to feel like a normal way of being.[1] There is a parable in which an older fish, swimming past a younger one, asks, "How's the water?" The younger fish replies, "What is water?" Like the fish, we can be unaware of the reality of what is all around us; when we feel overwhelmed and stressed all the time, experiences of burnout can come to feel like the "water" we're swimming in.

In some ways, burnout can feel like depression. It comes with the similar experience of complete exhaustion and the inability to get out of bed, where the thought of going through another day feels like a crushing weight on your chest or shoulders. It can also feel like overwhelm and stress, when there's simply too much to do in a single day, and you don't have the energy, motivation, or drive to tackle it all. Only a professional can help you tease out whether your exhaustion and lack of motivation are symptoms of depression or burnout, but the easiest way to distinguish burnout from depression is to consider whether or not you experience a lack of enjoyment of your hobbies. When you're burned out, you don't have time or energy to pursue passion projects or hobbies—but if you *do* engage with them, they are still enjoyable. When you're depressed, you cannot find any sense of pleasure or satisfaction even doing those hobbies you used to most enjoy. Burnout also tends to be centered around specific parts of our lives—like work—while depression is all-encompassing. In the earliest stages of my own burnout, I had no motivation or energy for my "day job," but I still had plenty of energy to pursue my other interests away from the office. That's the most classic example of burnout, and the one the World Health Organization (WHO) uses.

In 2019, the WHO specified in its definition of burnout that it is not a health condition in and of itself, but rather one that is specific to *workplace* stress, rather than other sources of stress. They clarify: "Burn-out is a syndrome conceptualized as resulting from chronic workplace stress that has not been successfully managed. . . . Burn-out refers specifically to phenomena in the occupational context and should not be applied to describe experiences in other areas of life."[2]

In this definition, the WHO specified three main characteristics of burnout:

1. Feelings of energy depletion or exhaustion

2. Depersonalization, or increased mental distance from one's job, or feelings of cynicism related to work

3. Reduced professional efficacy

While it's all well and good for the WHO to want to limit "burnout" to the workplace, that's not how language works. People use the term "burnout" to describe a wide range of feelings in a lot of contexts, and this usage reflects its lived reality. This specific focus on the workplace alone also does not address how life or stress actually work.

We don't experience our professional lives in the absence of the rest of reality. For example, eating dinner after working all day is a necessity. The work of meal planning and preparation constitute another "workload"; it can't be dismissed as a source of stress for the sake of a clean definition of "burnout." Constant exhaustion, feelings of depersonalization, and dissatisfaction can affect our work as parents, caregivers, students, and countless other roles that we play in our daily lives outside of our jobs, further impacting stress and burnout. The news cycle and anxieties about politics, race, public health, climate change, illness, war, violence, and economic situations also add to this ongoing overload of stress. Stress is the water we're swimming in, and burnout is the result of that stress.

Burnout is also a feature of late-stage capitalism—and I mean "feature" in the sense of the tech developer catchphrase, "It's not a bug, it's a feature." It's expected that high-performing workers (often reduced to the impersonal term "resources") will inevitably burn out in the current corporate climate. Unless a business is explicitly and intentionally choosing to follow sustainable business practices, at some point it is going to fall prey to the demand of the investors or shareholders for quarter-over-quarter growth. This growth-for-growth's-sake model is often arbitrary and extractive; in biology, the same model would be cancerous. As corporations grow more distant from the realities of everyday life, they care less and less about the impact of their activities on the environment (in fact, corporations contribute the most to climate change) or about the humans that make this financial growth happen. While the "brain drain" caused by losing employees to burnout can be expensive for businesses, they see this as a long-term net gain, because they can hire replacement workers at a lower salary—or not hire replacements at all. The shareholder and investment call to do more work with fewer people is a huge driver of layoffs and a huge cause of overwork and burnout.

Just as we are encouraged to reduce our individual carbon footprints while corporations freely create exponentially greater waste and greenhouse gas emissions, burnout is also framed as an individual problem. Many startups will frame burnout as a personal failing, telling a person who is burned out that they "couldn't hack it" in their "fast-paced" environment. Problems with leadership, organizational structure, documentation, and inconsistency across departments are often not scrutinized as a larger cause of burnout across a company

unless there is a legal liability. A pervasive atmosphere of "hustle culture" creates conditions for burnout, even if individual managers are
doing their best to prevent it.

This book is an approach to burnout recovery and prevention that
spans multiple contexts. It particularly aims at helping sufferers of
burnout who may have tried other strategies already but have found
that they just didn't seem to "take" or even work at all. The reasons
that some burnout-recovery approaches don't work for everyone
are as varied and unique as individuals. Sometimes, it simply doesn't
reach the unconscious emotions that are underlying burnout. Other
times, neurodivergence (diagnosed or undiagnosed) can create and
exacerbate burnout symptoms, and this aspect isn't getting properly
addressed.

The approach used in this book is rooted in two key theoretical
models: depth psychology and ecopsychology. *Depth psychology* pertains to reaching into the depths of our minds and hearts: the unconscious. The unconscious, as defined by Sigmund Freud (the founder
of psychoanalysis), is a personal collection of repressed memories,
dreams, aspects of self, and frustrations.[3] The personal unconscious
can appear in dreams, projections, and mirrored in other people
around us. Psychologist C. G. Jung took the concept of the unconscious in a different direction; while he, too, acknowledged a personal
unconscious, Jung delved into a *transpersonal* or collective version of
the unconscious. The transpersonal unconscious is not only available
to us in dreams but also reflected in myths, fairy tales, folk tales, and
symbolic systems like alchemy.[4] This approach is useful for burnout
recovery and prevention because it helps us to communicate with
our own personal unconscious in the language of metaphor—which
is what it understands. With depth psychology, we are better able to
learn from that unconscious, metaphorical material, and to tell the
personal unconscious what we need to change in the world around us
to be healthier and happier.

Ecopsychology is a subset of depth psychology. If depth psychology is the communication of unconscious material via the language of metaphor, then ecopsychology is the communication of unconscious material using environmental and ecological metaphors, specifically. In some senses, this use of an ecological metaphor can help us understand the connection between ourselves and our environment. Ecopsychology is also closely related to the *positive psychology* of Dr. Martin Seligman.[5] Positive psychology is a more recent revolution in psychology that shifts the treatment model from one of treating illness toward one of encouraging wellness. Whereas the classical treatment model for psychotherapy had been to eliminate symptoms in a patient, the positive psychology model is intended to move a person from the absence of symptoms into a state of thriving. It is my goal for this book to not only help readers recover from burnout but equip them with the tools they need to prevent future burnout.

Before digging into the practical chapters to come, I want to offer some of my own background and explain the reason I wrote this book. I experienced cycles of professional and personal burnout from 2016 to 2023. I say "cycles" because like many others, I managed to recover from burnout temporarily but found that it was always coming and going to some degree. Through the trial and error of seven years of professional burnout—which included going to graduate school and working full time—I have learned some keys to long-term success and long-term prevention of burnout.

In 2016, I began describing my digital marketing career as "soul-killing." Once satisfying, because it required my pattern-finding and data-analysis skills, the world of content strategy, search engine optimization, and technical website implementations had grown meaningless to me. When I did this work for the website WebMD, it felt like the work I did helped people. Yet I still felt like nothing I did made a difference. I oversaw my department at work, managing a team and ensuring that several big projects ran smoothly. It was a daily grind of ever-increasing responsibility and stress, with very few tangible rewards and no end in sight. There was no sense that "when this project is over, I will be able to relax"; no clear, finite end to the sprint that was being asked of me. Instead, it was a fast-paced marathon of work. Anyone who has gone for a run knows that's not sustainable—and an easy way to get injured.

I had an ever-increasing workload and number of people relying on me across the website-development, editorial, and marketing teams. At the same time, I was tackling the bulk of the mental load of housekeeping and homemaking. "Mental load" is defined as the unspoken thinking that goes into ensuring that a household runs smoothly—from creating home maintenance to-do lists to writing the grocery list. I was the breadwinner in our household, which meant that my job wasn't something I could afford to just step away from. There was no time for hobbies, personal passions, or creative pursuits. No matter how much I asked for help from my boss or my husband at the time, there was no real easing of the pressure. Any help I received was temporary and half-hearted.

Although I had signs of a chronic autoimmune condition as early as 1998, I wasn't diagnosed with one until a debilitating flare of psoriatic arthritis stopped me in my tracks in early 2017. The pain was devastating. I couldn't dress myself, let alone continue doing the bulk of the work at the office and at home. This chronic illness taught me several lessons about burnout, and hopefully I can pass those lessons on to readers before their bodies provide similarly painful instruction. Avoiding long-term illness is one of the biggest reasons to prioritize the prevention of chronic stress and burnout.

Chronic illness forced me to drop all the plates that I'd been spinning. When I quit my job, it took five people to handle the various projects I'd been working on. Where had that support been while I was still there, begging for help? Having five more people on my team could have prevented my burnout! When I was immobilized for several weeks with arthritis pain, the plates I spun within my household dropped, too. My then-husband had heard me asking for help, had heard me say that I couldn't do "everything," but because I continued doing everything, most of this work remained invisible to him. After a week or two of having to manage cooking, cleaning, laundry, pet care, and groceries, he was overwhelmed. He wasn't even doing *everything* I had been doing! He was just doing the bare minimum to make sure he had clean uniforms for work every day and no one starved. After processing his feelings of overwhelm, anger, and resentment, he was able to finally understand why I had been asking for help so often. The exercises and tactics in this book will help you hand off some of those spinning plates to others without dropping them in one loud crash to the floor. The idea is to effectively recruit the help you need earlier to prevent long-term damage to your relationships and health.

As I sought treatment for chronic illness and began my journey to recovering from burnout, I began working from home instead of the office. This was in 2017, so I had my experiences of cabin fever and work-from-home stress a few years before everyone else did during the "lockdowns" of the COVID-19 pandemic. However, like so many people discovered in 2020, I found that having control over some of the sensory elements of my environment was healing and helpful. This led me down several research paths—straight through to an autism diagnosis in 2020. While I deeply resonated with the descriptions of professional burnout, I discovered that I also had *autistic burnout*, as well.

Many members of the baby boomer, Generation X, and millennial age groups were diagnosed with neurodivergence (including apraxia or dyslexia, autism, or ADHD) only if they caused significant disruption in school and suffered terrible grades. But many high-achieving neurodivergent folks from these generations, particularly those who were raised as girls, were not diagnosed as children because their neurodivergence was not recognized. This means that not only do undiagnosed people lack key information about themselves and how to work more effectively in the world, but they also pay a very high cost in terms of burnout. Many of us in our thirties, forties, and older only consider getting a diagnosis after our children are diagnosed, as the increasing accuracy and frequency of childhood diagnosis inspires us to self-reflect. The online proliferation of descriptions of adult experiences of neurodivergence may also cause some adults to look into getting a late diagnosis. Sadly, it is the devastating breakdown caused by neurodivergent burnout that causes many of us to finally understand ourselves and our neurotypes. This was my experience.

For those of us who are neurodivergent, burnout can mean far more than exhaustion and cynicism. Neurodivergent burnout usually includes all the symptoms of professional burnout, plus the following:

- A loss of coping skills
- A regression of cognitive abilities
- A higher frequency of meltdowns
- Reduced tolerance of sensory input

Though this is a broad generalization, ADHD burnout tends to be relatively brief, but frequent. It generally means a complete shutdown at the end of the day, and an inability to engage with family, loved ones, or hobbies as a result. Its sibling, autistic burnout, tends to last for two to three years before sufferers begin to see new paths forward. This book, in large part, was inspired by conversations I have had within adult autistic communities regarding burnout recovery. The metaphorical approach that I offer is one in which many of my autistic friends were able to find a sense of hope and optimism.

In my own autistic burnout, I noticed that work that used to be easy for me no longer came so easily. I needed things to be quieter and darker (and then *even* quieter and *even* darker) to function in a space. Autistic meltdowns can look like angry outbursts or like panic attacks, and I had my share of both of those. I also lost a great deal of my ability to "mask," or to pretend to function gracefully in neurotypical society. Making eye contact grew more uncomfortable—to the point of being intolerable. And my ability to "fake it" with social niceties dropped to nearly nonexistent levels. The layer of autistic burnout on top of my professional burnout made working not just difficult and meaningless, but downright torturous. Unfortunately, many adults must experience the devastation of neurodivergent burnout before it becomes apparent that we may not be neurotypical. This book speaks to this journey and raises this possibility for those who may have never considered neuro-divergence in their own lives.

After I started working from home, I also began seriously pursuing a passion project and enrolled in graduate school. In the PhD program for Mythological Studies with Emphasis in Depth Psychology at Pacifica Graduate Institute, I was able to learn and grow in new directions, separately from my career. This program focuses a great deal on understanding myths and folktales as metaphors and on using metaphors as psychological road maps for how to function in the world. What I offer in this book is a rich, complex ecological metaphor that helps me to conceptualize burnout, recovery, and prevention in a real and tangible way.

The metaphor that we will explore is that of wildfire. In addition to my lived experience of professional burnout and of physical and autistic burnout, I have also experienced a wildfire. In 2022, the largest wildfire in New Mexico history reached within one and a half miles of my house—a house I had purchased just four months earlier. This was the Hermit's Peak / Calf Canyon wildfire, and I continue to live in and among its scars. I watched the efforts to contain it, and I pursue an ongoing effort to maintain fire safety on my property and around my home. Climate change has resulted in more frequent and destructive wildfires that burn more acreage and are harder to fight; wildfire is a lived reality for an increasing number of people, and it's very close to home for me.

Wildfire is not just a one-time event of active burning. After the fires have gone out, there is the flooding of terrain that is now unprotected from erosion. After the floods have passed, small plant life begins to grow in the burn scar, and animals begin to return. Then, efforts must be made to prevent the delicate scar from igniting again. Burn scars are among the most susceptible to reignition, so they must be carefully tended. If it's not already clear how this metaphor applies to burnout in people, it will be.

In the next chapter, I will explain the wildfire metaphor and how it parallels the psychological cycles of burnout. Chapter 2 applies these lessons to professional burnout and works through the stages of recovery when the workplace is the main source of chronic stress. For those who think something may be going on beyond professional burnout, chapter 3 delves into the process and recovery steps for neurodivergent burnout. Chapter 4 then addresses other systemic, cultural, and real-life causes of burnout that usually go unaddressed but are part of the "water" we swim in in our daily lives. The final chapter focuses on long-term burnout prevention, resilience, and self-care.

Within each chapter there are journaling exercises and activities. These are tools to help readers discover their own unacknowledged sources of stress, their emotions, and their unconscious needs. In the world of depth psychology, we speak a great deal about how the powerful unconscious mind does not understand the difference between actions taken in symbolic form and those taken in real life. You can trick your unconscious into supporting big shifts in your external world by physically doing small symbolic acts. The activities in this book are designed to communicate with the unconscious on a psychological level. The journaling prompts make the unconscious material more consciously recognized. They are devised to allow new emotional and psychological information to bubble up to the surface. For this reason, I strongly recommend having a private, dedicated notebook, computer file, or blank journal for this work. The combination of journal exercises and physical activities are intended to support you from the "bottom up," as opposed to a "top-down" approach that starts with cognitive understanding but may not be conscious or able to be embodied fully.

Like wildfires, burnout can be overwhelming, devastating, and catastrophic. But there is an element of optimism to be found in the wake of its destruction. My hope is that this book helps readers see that spark of hope for their own burnout recovery and find a clear path to both recovery and prevention of future burnout.

A Note on Mental Health, Trauma, and Other Relevant Concerns

This book is intended to address the problems associated with burnout. Professional burnout and workplace stress do not occur without household, cultural, and other forms of stress. Neurodivergent burnout, chronic illness, systemic racism, and other factors that create burnout do not exist in a vacuum. We have homes, families, and lives which may both provide support and be stressful themselves. We also may have symptoms from previous traumatic experiences which are made worse by burnout and stress.

Like stress, burnout is not in and of itself a diagnosis of mental illness. However, it's not unusual to seek treatment for generalized anxiety or chronic depression amid burnout. The exercises in this book are intended to be undertaken along with support from a trained and licensed mental-health professional, such as a counselor through your workplace Employee Assistance Plan (EAP) or a regularly visited therapist or licensed clinical social worker (LCSW). This portion of your support should not be neglected, and if medication is warranted, then that can also help. However, burnout can look a lot like depression, and long-term medication can sometimes mask long-term burnout. Discuss your burnout with your prescribing doctor to ensure that you're getting the right treatment for your circumstances.

Past trauma, too, creates a unique situation vis-a-vis burnout. *Trauma* refers to any event that a person has been unable to metabolize or process fully, or that they have been unable to contextualize in the larger story of their life or how the world works. In *The Inner World of Trauma,* Donald Kalsched examines more traditional definitions of trauma as experiences of "unbearable psychic pain or anxiety" through the unconscious responses of symbol, metaphor, and story.[6] He writes, "The psyche cannot metabolize its own experience and render it meaningful."[7] Traumatic events get stuck in the present tense, rather than in the past, until we can process the emotions and circumstances around them—which sometimes can be very difficult to do. Traumatic memories can "spark" the burnout wildfire and exacerbate it, making it very difficult to exit the burnout cycle and recover fully. It is important to discuss the possible coexistence of trauma and burnout with your mental-health provider, as they will be able to help you to navigate your own unique situation.

CHAPTER 1

The Wildfire Metaphor and Where You Are Within the Burnout Cycle

THIS BOOK USES an extended metaphor of the wildfire cycle in the natural world to help provide a psychological road map for recovery and long-term healing from burnout. The use of metaphors to help us understand a complicated situation is not a new concept. Myths, folktales, and literature have been doing this since the dawn of humanity.

One of the most well-known and common metaphors used in storytelling and modern media is the "Hero's Journey," a concept made famous by the writer Joseph Campbell. Campbell identified a common story occurring in a wide range of cultural myths, involving a heroic journey to an unknown world and triumphant return—think *Star Wars* or *Moana*. In addition to his analysis of what he calls "the monomyth," Campbell outlined four functions of myth and metaphor, which he revisited and clarified over his body of work.[1] The first function is a mystical and metaphysical one: myths are intended to create and instill a sense of awe and wonder at the mystery of life. The second function is cosmological, explaining how real life and individual experience is tied to the larger mystery of existence. The third function is to validate, support, and reinforce the social rules and roles that we play within that faith structure.[2]

These three functions of myth do not easily apply to our wildfire metaphor, as the way we will use it in this book to explain burnout could be considered more pragmatic and down-to-earth. However, the fourth function, as outlined by Campbell, is precisely what we're going after. He describes the fourth function as "pedagogical," later calling it a "psychological function." By this, he means that myths and metaphors can teach us "how to live a human lifetime under any circumstances."[3] In *The Hero's Journey*, Campbell expanded upon this by describing the psychological function of myth as "the guiding of individuals in a harmonious way through the inevitable crises of a lifetime."[4] Essentially, myths and metaphors can provide a psychological road map for us: They help us define what story we are currently in, and where precisely we are within it. With that information, we are better able to anticipate the next steps we must take. This is why and how this book is organized around metaphor.

The process of using a metaphor as a psychological road map is relatively straightforward. Using your own physical symptoms, dream images, and emotions, we will be able to identify where you are in the story. Dropping a "you are here" pin on the map helps us to understand the next step forward, the conditions that must be met to move on from where you are, which landmarks to watch for, and which turns to take. Metaphor also provides a glimpse of possible futures and helps us envision what will happen beyond the next curve in the road.

One of the first steps is to *embody* the stage in the story where you find yourself, or to act out the feelings and sensations associated with it. By embodying emotions or metaphorical stages, we are better able to move through them. The following chapters include practical rituals or activities to help your body process the work you are doing.

The unconscious mind, which we are trying to work with, does not differentiate activities that are done in real life from those done within a "ritual" context. By doing small acts intentionally, we can teach our bodies and minds important lessons. By doing this work "from the bottom up," so to speak, you will be working with the powerful stuff of the unconscious toward your own healing.

In this book, we will be using the ecological metaphor of wildfire to address conscious and unconscious emotions and needs relating to burnout. To apply this metaphor accurately, we need to define the stages of wildfire, describe its conditions, and explore the specifics of its ecology.

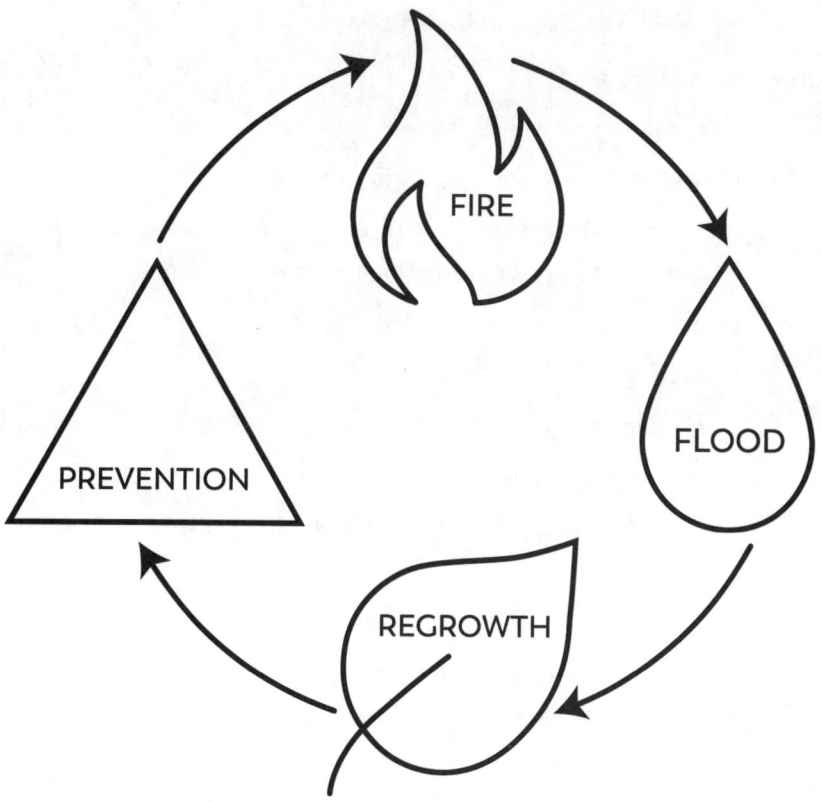

The wildfire/burnout process.

Before I describe each part of the wildfire process and its meta-phorical applications, we first need to place your "you are here" pin on the map. The following exercise is intended to help you identify your current stage of burnout.

Questionnaire: Identifying Your Current Stage of Burnout

For each item, score how true each statement is for you right now, with 1 meaning "not at all true" and 5 meaning "very true."

- My work feels meaningless.
- I don't feel like I can get a good night's sleep.
- My eating habits are getting worse and worse.
- I often feel hopeless.
- I feel out of control of my life.
- I fantasize about quitting my job in a dramatic fashion.
- Even though I'm unhappy at work, I don't even bother looking for another job; it won't be any better anywhere else.
- I don't have time for myself or my hobbies.
- I feel exhausted all the time.
- I feel cynical and jaded about my work.
- I don't feel like I'm any good at my job anymore.
- My manager has spoken with me about the decreased quality of my work lately.
- I feel like I'm at the end of my rope.
- I use up all my energy at work, and I don't have any patience left for my family at the end of the day.
- I don't really care about my work.
- I'm afraid my job is making me a worse person.

- I feel like I'm "spinning my wheels"; it doesn't feel like I'm achieving anything at work.

- I don't have any close relationships with coworkers or teammates.

- My job feels "soul sucking" and leaves me emotionally drained.

- All the people I was close to at work have left or were laid off.

Scoring: Add your numbers together to determine your likely stage.

- If you scored between 20 and 35: You are most likely in the Regrowth stage of burnout. You probably recognize earlier stages of your burnout experience in a number of the statements above, but you are not immediately caught up in it now.

- If you scored between 36 and 65: This is tricky, because a score in this range could mean that you're either in the Flood stage or in the Prevention stage. It's going to be up to you to identify where you were before and where you feel like you're heading.

- If you scored over 66: You are most likely in the Fire stage of burnout. The anger you may feel in this stage is a critical emotional signal that something needs to change in your life right now.

Map in hand, let's explore the larger terrain of the wildfire process and what it can teach us about burnout.

Circumstances Creating Wildfire

In most ecosystems, wildfire is a way that forests regulate themselves. A lightning strike can create a fire that clears underbrush and renews the forest floor. Small, regularly occurring fires can prevent larger wildfires in later seasons. In our burnout metaphor, "healthy" fire might look like brief periods of dissatisfaction, exhaustion, and stress which are alleviated by a vacation or the completion of a project. It can signal a needed course-correction, prompting you to ask for different tasks at work or take up a new hobby. Unfortunately, like this form of wildfire, this form of stress is becoming increasingly rare.

Circumstances that turn small fires into big ones are part of our changing global climate. Droughts, unusually warm temperatures, and extremely high winds can create catastrophic wildfires. With increasing frequency, those living in areas with wildfires are experiencing the climate crisis year-round. Here in New Mexico, the wildfire season is in late winter and early spring. After snows have ceased and before monsoon season begins in May or June, the temperatures and winds are high and the dry, dead plant life is essentially tinder. In addition to driving more wildfires, climate change is also a source of external stress that affects our daily lives and can create burnout. But there are many other sources: The global pandemic of COVID-19, for example, has created fractures in supply chains and healthcare systems, impacting the health of countless people and even leading to death. (There will be more about long COVID in chapter 4). In the corporate world, the demand for greater profits with reduced staff is increasing workloads and stress levels across all sectors. Concerns about the rising cost of housing and food act as "high winds," making feelings of professional burnout bleaker, because we know we must continue working to make enough money to survive.

Drought is an interesting metaphor. Droughts that occur over years can dry out the trees themselves, making them more susceptible to burning. The lack of rain, snow, and ground water creates a landscape that is ready to burn. Metaphorically, water is usually a symbol for emotions. In this case, I see water as *meaning*. If our work is meaningful, we get enough "rain" to help stave off the devastation of burnout for a longer period of time. In Martin Seligman's book *Flourish*, he describes a meaningful life as "belonging to and serving something you believe is bigger than the self."[5] Teachers, healthcare workers, and public-safety workers often find a great deal of meaning in their work, which fuels and sustains their higher stress levels and longer hours. When our work feels meaningful, we're less likely to succumb to burnout, just as when the trees are full of sap and the ground water is plentiful, a forest is less likely to catch fire. But this does not mean that wildfires *can't* occur. In fact, some of these more meaningful types of work can generate some of the longest and most cyclical journeys into and out of burnout.

In some parts of the country, government agencies try to prevent the devastation of large wildfires by lighting "controlled burns," specifically chosen areas of wilderness that are temporarily ignited for the health of the landscape. But in the case of the Hermit's Peak/Calf Canyon fires, both sparks that started the five-hundred-thousand-acre burn were from "controlled" burns that got out of control. It may seem sustainable to stave off catastrophic burnout by living from one vacation to the next, or even one weekend to the next, for a few years. However, this kind of pace can lead to burnout very easily. Recognizing if you're going from one controlled burn to the next is an important part of acting to create long-term change and prevention. One physical symptom of this can be instantly coming down with a mysterious illness or bug whenever you get a week off or an extended break. Stress can keep illness at bay for short periods of time, but when stress levels drop, our bodies are especially susceptible to illness and infections. If you get a sniffle every time you get a four-day weekend away from work, you are likely at high risk of burnout.

Some plants and landscapes *require* fire to germinate. There are certain flowers and trees that only produce new life if they have been burned. Under the conditions of small, relatively contained fires that help maintain a healthy ecosystem, these plants thrive. This might look like a person who exceeds expectations and accomplishes mighty feats or high productivity at work. It might be strokes of brilliance that are spurred by a little positive stress (also known as *eustress*). This may be a great source of engagement, or *flow*, for you—which is a vital part of a resilient and happy life. However, if demands continue to mount and there aren't preventive measures in place, then these kinds of "burns" can be high risk. They bring with them the potential danger of the spread of fire to other areas of life.

When the Fire Is Burning

The language of burnout is already the language of fire and flame. The metaphors and figures of speech we use in our daily lives may also reflect this. "I just want to burn it all down," "just watch the world burn," "burn the candle at both ends," and "don't burn your bridges" are a few phrases that leap to mind when we're consumed by the fires of burnout.

Wildfires spread quickly, and depending on the direction of the winds, they can threaten homes and towns. They choke the air with smoke, displace wildlife, and turn the sky an eerie orange. People living in the vicinity of the fire have to pack their bags and cars to be ready to evacuate at a moment's notice. Homeowners might need to partner with local firefighters to ensure that their houses are not at risk of burning.

When a wildfire is actively burning and the air is thick with smoke, we are focused only on our own survival. When I was watching fire maps as the fire spread, and my yard was crowded with disheveled, tired-looking deer, I barely noticed how much my body was in fight/flight mode. My survival instinct was activated, and anxiety climbed. I find now that when I smell brushfire smoke, that fear returns. This adrenalized state of being is vital for short-term survival, providing us with the fuel to get ourselves safely out of the path of the blaze. But when the "fire" is workload or stress, that short-term survival fuel will eventually run out. Some of the practices in the following chapters are aimed at getting out of this physical state of fear.

There is often collateral damage when we are in a burned-out state. Our relationships may suffer. We might get into car accidents due to road rage or inattention. We might have outsized stress responses to ordinary, everyday events and aggravations. This fallout is inevitable when we leave ourselves to burn unchecked. When wildfire is in a forest area without roads or buildings, firefighters use bulldozers, fire, and water to create "containment" lines—places where they determine the fire will not pass. They use mounded earth and other tools to prevent fires from reaching populated areas. Similarly, if burnout is left uncontained, it can stretch into the rest of our lives and relationships.

When It Finally Rains, It Floods

Though firefighters work to contain wildfires and protect structures, there's not much they can do about acres of forest that are burning unchecked. They can drop moisture into the air to help slow the spread, but much of the forest simply must burn. The two things that put out wildfires are a lack of fuel and the arrival of rain.

Wildfires run out of fuel when everything has burned down to ash, when the soil has been burned several inches down, and when nothing remains in the burn scar. This only occurs in the hottest parts of the fire and is relatively rare. This rarity is good, because this type of burn takes a very long time to recover from. In burnout, a "lack of fuel" might mean no longer having physical energy or ability to continue working. It may be a chronic illness, autoimmune problems, long COVID, or some other form of physical disability. It is my sincere hope that this book helps prevent others from getting to that point.

The better, healthier option to put out a wildfire is rain. However, rain, too, comes with danger. When it finally rains in New Mexico, it pours. Monsoon season is characterized by frequent, sudden, heavy thunderstorms in one isolated place at a time. These torrential downpours—often dumping several inches of rain in a matter of minutes—is usually too much for the landscape to absorb. The acequias, arroyos, and rivers swell with run-off water. When the snow on the mountaintop melts, it too, runs into the waterways. Again, water usually signifies emotional content in depth psychology. In the case of burnout, the main emotions of the Flood stage are sadness and grief. Grieving the life we had before burnout is a difficult process. It's hard to give ourselves the time and space to grieve. Often, people reenter the burnout cycle when they do not allow this part to happen.

When there is no undergrowth on the forest floor to absorb and slow the flow of water, the water speeds up and flows even faster into the waterways. It captures the debris created by the fire. Ash, branches, and fallen trees all run into the waterways with the floods. (This is one of the greatest dangers of living in the scar of a recent wildfire.) In the Flood stage of the burnout process, this may look like disappointing others, missing important family events, or taking more sick time away from work. Debris and ash can also clog waterways, which in the burnout process might mean bottled-up, unaddressed emotions. In this stage, having psychological and social support is most critical.

When the rain floods the forest floor unchecked, depending upon the composition of the soil, another danger is mudslides. Where there are no roots of plants to help keep the soil in place, the earth itself slides away with the water. Mudslides are fast, dangerous, and deadly. They can engulf cars, houses, and communities. Metaphorically speaking, mudslides are another part of coping with the emotional aftermath of burnout. We may change or lose important relationships in our lives if mudslides happen in our burnout journeys. If we aren't working with our supervisors closely through this part of the process, this stage is when we are at the highest risk for being laid off or put on performance-improvement plans at work. While losing a job can be seen as an opportunity to change direction, doing so unexpectedly can cause even more stress in the middle of burnout recovery. (Some people may have come to this book following such a layoff.) In the event of losing a job suddenly, it's necessary to take stock of what's still standing; this is absolutely the Flood stage of the work.

New Life and Regrowth

When the rain stops coming so frequently, the debris is cleared from waterways, and the mudslide damage has been assessed, then the landscape can begin to regrow. One of the most important things to know about the regrowth process is that burn scars permanently change the forest where they happen. Different plants grow, and different trees appear. You will see oaks where pines once stood. They can take years to achieve a new canopy, but again, the composition of that canopy will be different from what it once was.

One of the most important parts of grieving following a wildfire is letting go of the forest that was once there, acknowledging that it will never be the same and that some things will never come back. There are old trees that used to hold up the canopy and stand guard over the forest, but they may not have survived the blaze. Similarly, once we start to recover from the Fire and Flood stages of a burnout, to lean on our old skill sets is to court disaster. While it is possible to stay in the same career—even at the same company—and recover from burnout, it is *not* possible to return to the same level of workload or productivity. To get out of the burnout cycle, you will have to fundamentally change how you work and how you think about work.

One of the first crews to enter the burn scar goes in to assess the damage. They look at which large trees and portions of the canopy survived. They look at where the fire did not reach very deeply into the soil, and where some seeds and plants will likely sprout right away. Following the devastation of burnout, we have to take this inventory within ourselves. Which interests and skills still stand and grow? Where do we still have the fertile soil of curiosity? There are exercises in the following chapters to help us with this assessment and self-discovery.

The regrowth process is a slow one. It requires many small plants to sprout, birds and insects to drop seeds on the bare soil, fungus and mushrooms to help with the decay of the ash and debris. With the canopy burned, more sunlight reaches the forest floor, which allows different plants to grow. Some plants prefer disturbed soil, and they begin to sprout. An example of this is an herb called *mullein*. It's amazing that mullein grows so soon after a fire, because it's used medicinally for lung conditions—nature knows that we need to recover from smoke inhalation. Mullein can also be used to treat grief, making it an important plant for the Regrowth stage of the burnout process, as well. In this stage, we are beginning to sense new life. We may feel like we are finally coming back to ourselves. By allowing the sun to shine on long-dormant hopes and dreams, and by allowing new ideas to sprout, we begin to see new possibilities.

Regrowth is a slow process. Just as the regrowth of the forest is intermittently interrupted by summer rains, we may cycle back to grief and sorrow at this stage, perhaps as we realize there are more aspects of our old lives that we must let go of. It's critical to maintain both patience and curiosity as new, small things sprout in our lives.

Wildfire Prevention

In an ideal world, we would have done all the work to prevent wildfires before they happen at all. Unfortunately, in many cases, we do not realize we are at risk of burning out until we have already begun to experience it. In this case, we must work harder to prevent future cases of burnout, because wildfire burn scars are very susceptible to igniting again in later seasons. Fires in burn scars can move faster and destroy more in their paths. They are among the most dangerous kinds of wildfires. Burnout on top of previous burnout—where we cycle through layers of burnout over and over again—can also cause similar devastation. While we might escape permanent chronic illness or disability following the first few "burns," we might not after the next one. For this reason, active prevention of burnout (and wildfires) is absolutely necessary.

Living in a wildfire zone, I have to think about the safety and resilience of my property, first. The way to do this is to think in concentric circles around the home. "Hardening" the house itself from fire includes things like stucco repair and limiting the flammable objects on or against the house. (I replaced the wood mulch in flower beds with rocks, for example.) Then, I need to assess fire risks within ten feet of the house. Then a ring of thirty feet, then fifty feet. I need to look at my evacuation routes and the evacuation routes of my neighbors. And I need to trim the trees and maintain the health of the forest on my property. This is not a one-time set of actions; I keep fire safety in mind all year, every year. Burnout prevention is very similar: it includes the ongoing setting and reinforcing of boundaries between work and home life, between what is possible to do and what is too much. It also includes maintaining constant, regular communication channels with others that help us remain safe during times of stress.

Wildfire safety also means keeping my fire-evacuation kits refreshed and up-to-date, filled with all the necessities to get out of the house immediately in the event of a future fire. I need to know where cat carriers, food, and emergency supplies are so I can find them at a moment's notice. Batteries need to be refreshed and contact lists updated. This element of preparatory self-care, both physical and emotional, is also critical for burnout prevention. We should always keep our own needs in our sights and be able to identify what might be potential problems for us.

As mentioned earlier, controlled burns are often used to help prevent larger wildfires. In our own lives, controlled burns may look like finite projects with clear end dates. They may also be daily sprints of engagement or flow, which is vital for our personal feelings of success and satisfaction. While repeated burns and burns without proper containment can cause out-of-control wildfires, there's nothing inherently wrong with fire itself. Likewise, the trick to burnout prevention is to ensure that you have stress-mitigating practices and support in place, so that when stress occurs, it doesn't get out of control or last for too long.

CHAPTER 2

Applying the Wildfire Metaphor to Professional Burnout

NOW THAT WE'VE FULLY EXPLORED how wildfire can be understood as a metaphor for burnout, we will apply that metaphor to real life—specifically, to professional burnout. (We will cover other forms of burnout later in the book, as well as other potential sources of stress or feelings that may exacerbate professional burnout.) You may have already identified where you are located within the wildfire cycle in your own experience of burnout (see page 16). If not, there will be a series of exercises and activities in this chapter to help you determine your current place in the cycle. The activities provided are an important part of communicating with your unconscious through action and imagination. We need to engage the unconscious parts of our minds to better speed and facilitate healing and create lasting change.

However, the level of self-examination required for this part of the process is deeper than some people may be comfortable with. This isn't easy work. So I want to start by offering a handful of tools that will support and guide you along the way. The most important part of this process is assembling your support team. Burnout isn't easy; it's a hard thing to experience, and an even harder thing to recover from. No one fights wildfire alone, so be sure to assemble your team in advance and check in with them often.

Your firefighting team should include the people living in your house and—in a perfect world—your manager or supervisor at work. If your burnout support team can also include someone from a workplace Employee Assistance Plan (EAP) or a therapist with whom you have an established relationship, that is ideal. EAPs are part of most corporate health-benefits packages in the United States but are underutilized.[1] We don't often hear about them (or remember they are there), but they can provide confidential counseling, referrals to therapists, and other mental-health support services at low or no cost to the employee—without alerting employers or managers. Because of the stigma around mental health, sometimes HR teams don't highlight the availability of this valuable resource.

Your support team has a few different jobs, and it's okay to delegate the work according to the skills and abilities of each member of your team as well as the relationships you have with them. It is best if you have:

- Someone who can understand your emotions, reflect them back to you, and validate your experience—preferably without rushing to offer solutions. (This is where that EAP counselor or therapist is useful.)
- Someone who can help you have fun and play. Friends, kids, and pets are great for this. Lean on these team members to get exercise, enjoy the sunshine, and take breaks.
- Someone who can help you prioritize tasks and reduce the amount of stuff that's expected of you. Managers and spouses both fall into this category. By being honest about your burnout and asking for help, you can often find ways to reduce your overall workload. This can help you create more time for yourself and your recovery.

There are, of course, dozens of other types of support that can be useful here. Accountability partners, peers, and coworkers who have been through a similar experience can all be helpful, as well as social media and other forms of social support. Your team will be vital as we move forward in this process.

EMPOWER WORK *at www.empowerwork.org offers a free text line with trained peer counselors to help people in the US navigate tough situations at work. To get confidential support, text "HELLO" to 510-674-1414.*

You are going to need a journal for the exercises in this chapter. I recommend purchasing an inexpensive composition notebook or using an empty notebook you already have on hand. It can be a fancy journal or a simple spiral notebook; the point is that your work should be in one single place, so that you can refer to previous exercises as you go. Be sure that this dedicated journal is kept private from loved ones, as this is your personal space for processing difficult emotions. The more private your journal is kept, the safer the space is for you to share your unconscious truths.

The first exercise I recommend beginning right away, and continuing well into your recovery, is called "Three Good Things."[2] This is a positive psychology practice in which, at the beginning of each day, you write down three good things that happened the day before. If nothing good happened at all, then write down something that could have gone much worse. This practice is supported by a lot of neuroscience research. It helps rewire your brain to look for daily good events instead of problems to solve, which can relieve some depressive emotions. Gratitude journaling is a similar practice, but I find "Three Good Things" to be a little emotionally easier to do during burnout; gratitude can wait until we are in the prevention phase.

EXERCISE
Three Good Things

For the next month, commit to writing down Three Good Things each morning in your journal (or any place you can access daily), listing events from the day before. It can just be a few words or phrases, as long as you know what they mean. There are no limits or requirements for what constitutes a "good thing." If you cannot think of three good things that happened, then list things that could have gone worse but didn't.

Example entry:

Three Good Things: Monday, October 3

1. I got a good night's sleep.

2. I got a phone call from Marcia.

3. When the dog got out, at least he came right back to me instead of running all over the neighborhood.

(In this example, the third item is an example of something that "could have gone worse.")

In addition to writing down "Three Good Things" as a daily practice, you may find yourself journaling more often than you ordinarily would. Feel free to use your journal in any way that supports your recovery, whether that is venting and processing emotions, making notes for therapy conversations, or channeling your frustrations into cartoons or doodles.

Identifying Where You Are in the Wildfire Process

The questionnaire in the previous chapter may have already helped you understand where you are in the burnout process. It's likely that some of the stages of the process were very familiar to you, while others were unfamiliar or sounded strange. This process is more of a spiral than it is a pure circle—you will be looping back to previous stages again and again throughout the process of recovery. Don't get discouraged if you discover you are earlier in the process than you originally thought.

As you progress through the stages of Fire, Flood, Regrowth, and Prevention, your psyche should tell you where you are. Are there any recurring images in recent dreams that relate to this metaphor? If so, make a note of those images in your journal. Dream images are among the most personal, accurate, and powerful guideposts along this journey. Keeping a dream journal is an excellent practice during this process, as it can signal when you've switched from one stage of the burnout process to the next. For example, when I started dreaming of rivers and swamps instead of houses burning down, I knew I had moved from the "Fire" to "Flood" phase in my own burnout cycle. Dream journals do not have to be flowery or overly interpretive. Simply noting down a few words about the overarching feeling, theme, or images that you remember is plenty to guide you on the journey.

Think about your conversations in recent days and weeks. Are there any metaphors, figures of speech, or turns of phrase that you would use more frequently than others to describe how you feel? For example, if you find yourself saying things like "watching the world burn" or "burning bridges," you are likely in the "Fire" phase. But if you are using phrases like "planting seeds" or "sprouting" you may be in the "Recovery" phase. Ask members of your support team if they have noticed any phrases becoming more common in your speech or texts.

Another way to access your unconscious mind and its messages is to speed-write. This practice is repeated in several exercises in this book because it can trick your brain into getting out of the way. This is a great way to uncover hidden fears, motivations, and emotions.

EXERCISE
Identifying Feelings

In your journal, write down a list of numbers from one to ten. As fast as you can, complete the following sentence ten times. "In my burnout process, I feel _____."

Now read through your list and circle the lines that resonate the most with how you feel. Classic burnout symptoms include exhaustion, cynicism, helplessness, and feelings of meaninglessness and despair. These emotions may be present in many of the stages to a greater or lesser degree. However, when expanding the burnout model to encompass Regrowth and Prevention, the emotional landscape changes. Each stage has a few predominant underlying feelings.

- The Fire stage is dominated by ANGER.
- The Flood stage is dominated by GRIEF.
- The Regrowth stage is dominated by CURIOSITY, NEW JOY, and possibly even HOPE.
- The Prevention stage is dominated by DETERMINATION or STRENGTH.

It's okay if it's not easy to pinpoint these feelings exactly. Emotional processes are not linear, and they do not follow logical patterns quite so neatly. It's possible to be in the Fire and Flood stage at the same time, or to move rapidly back and forth between them. If you are only in the early stages of burnout, you may be in the Prevention stage of the emotional experience—determined to not let the whole forest catch fire.

One way to approach this chapter is to identify where you are *right now*, today, and address the exercises and elements of the metaphor relating just to that stage. Another way to approach it is to start at the beginning of the process and move systematically through each stage. This allows you to fully process and metabolize each part before moving on to the next. I recommend a combination of these two approaches, if you have enough time. Remember, you can always revisit the exercises tomorrow, or the day after that, or whenever it feels right. In the next several sections, we will cover what each stage feels like in depth, and what you can do to process, heal, and recover from burnout.

When You're in the Fire Itself

The predominant emotion of the Fire stage of burnout is anger. Anger is an emotional signal that something in your current circumstance needs to change. Anger is a sign that a boundary of the self and soul has been violated, and it demands correction. But when paired with a feeling of helplessness, this anger is often not expressed, acknowledged, or processed. Rather than exploding outwards, this type of anger is more implosive. It can then turn into sarcasm, resentment, avoidance, cynicism, and disconnection from the people you work with or for. Feelings of unfairness, being passed over, or injustice are subtle forms of anger. It's important to get in touch with your anger, because it is the fuel that keeps the fire of burnout going. Stress may be a hot, dry wind that spreads the flames, but it is anger that speeds their destruction.

Remember, wildfire doesn't care what it's burning. It displaces animals, burns endangered plants, threatens homes, and kills canopies of trees that took hundreds of years to grow. It finds fuel, and it burns fuel. This is what the fiery anger of burnout can do in your life. It may be fueled by problems at work right now, but if that fire is left unattended, a spark usually comes home with you at the end of the day. It can destroy relationships, disrupt routines, and take your energy away from hobbies or recreational activities.

But anger can also fuel recovery. By feeling, expressing, and processing anger in an honest way, and by creating appropriate boundaries, you can "fireproof" important areas of your life.

EXERCISE
I'm So Angry

In your journal, number a page from one to ten, and as quickly as you can, complete the following sentence: "I'm so angry that _____."

Read through your list of answers. Which one surprises you? Which one makes you feel guilty? Write a longer entry about two or three answers that stand out the most, or speak about them with your mental-health provider.

Anger is often a signal that something in your life needs to change. Return to the list of things you're angry about, and add to each one the following: The thing that needs to change in this situation is _____.

When we think about things that need to change, the next step is to assess whether we have any control or influence over the change that needs to happen. Having **control** over a situation means having the power to say "no" to something or the ability to shift your own behavior. Having **influence** over a situation means that while you may not be able to control it, you can still ask for help in changing it. For example, if you are angry that the kitchen is always a mess, you first need to look at your own contributions to the mess. These are elements you can control: You can put your own dishes in the dishwasher, and you can take out the trash when it needs to be emptied. However, if you live with other people, it's possible that their dishes and trash are the cause of the mess. In this case, you do not have control, but you *do* have influence. You can calmly explain to them how the mess in the kitchen is causing you extra stress, and you can work together to divide chores, set timelines for actions, and take individual responsibility.

EXERCISE
Control and Influence

Return to your list of things that need to change. Now, add this to each item:

I have control over _____.

I have influence over _____.

I have to let go of _____.

The thing I will do right now is _____.

It is important to **do** the thing that you have listed here. You show yourself you are trustworthy and act with integrity when you do those things. This is what we must implement in order to recover from burnout.

With this exercise, you've acknowledged your anger and used its energy to come up with a realistic next step. This process also addresses the feelings of overwhelm and helplessness that come with this stage. Please note that sometimes there are things that make us angry that we have no control or influence over. This means that we must let them go. We can acknowledge and feel our anger about the situation, but we must be realistic about what we can do.

Frequently, anger is triggered by a boundary violation of some kind. Boundaries are our personal limits, the lines we draw around our physical, mental, and emotional space and time. My favorite way to conceptualize boundaries is to think about property lines. If you have a house and a plot of land, you have an imaginary line where your property ends and the property of your neighbor begins. Fences sometimes mark this line, but they often don't extend all the way to the sidewalk or road. If some kids are playing basketball in the driveway next door, and their ball lands on your lawn, you're not likely to get super angry about it. If a neighbor's dog pees on your grass, might just shrug it off. But if the kids set up a picnic on your lawn, that's not okay. If the dog decides that your front yard is its personal toilet, and no one cleans it up, you're likely to put up a sign or holler at the neighbor. Sometimes, it's the repeated, ongoing violation of a boundary that makes it infuriating. And some boundaries are more permeable than others: We are more forgiving of a stray baseball in the yard than we are one that smashes through a bedroom window.

When it comes to burnout, these boundary violations might look like expectations of working after hours or on weekends, a bigger workload without additional pay, or having reasonable breaks—like lunch breaks—routinely booked over.

EXERCISE
Boundary Violations

Make a list of personal boundaries that are currently being violated. (Hint: Your "angry" list probably points to some or most of them!)

As mentioned above, anger in burnout is often accompanied by a sense of helplessness. The people who violate your boundaries may have authority over you at work, or your financial situation may dictate whether or not you can risk retaliation from your employer if you set firmer boundaries. However, that sense of helplessness is often *global*, applied to everything across the board. In this case, we want to look at the *small* things we can change within ourselves and in our daily lives. The most important thing to remember about anger is that it is energy from within; it is intended to fuel change, to make something happen in a different way.

EXERCISE
Establishing Boundaries

Choose from the list of boundary violations the two or three that make you the angriest, the ones that fire you up the most. Now, think of small, reasonable things that you could do to reassert or re-establish your boundaries—perhaps things you see other coworkers already modeling, or things you often wish you could "get away with." Examples might include:

- I will turn off notifications on Slack and email after hours.

- I will change my lunch break to "out of office" in my calendar.

- I won't accept extra shifts anymore.

Now here's the hard part: Use the emotional and energetic fuel of your anger to actually do one of those things.

If establishing better boundaries includes changing how you're working, it's a good idea to let a supervisor or manager know. For example, you might say, "Just a heads-up: I'm trying to avoid getting really burned out, so I'm not going to be available to answer emails or messages over the weekend anymore." You don't have to explain any further than that; this helps reset the expectations they may have of you without creating problems later. This is why your manager or supervisor is a critical member of your support team. Employers don't want to lose good employees, so managing and preventing burnout should be something that they *want* to help with—but they may not really know how. This kind of boundary setting helps them understand what would work best for you.

Many jobs don't offer leeway for setting those kinds of boundaries. Servers must serve food when there are customers ready to order. Healthcare providers aren't always able to plan what a shift might look like ahead of time. Still, be sure to know your rights at work. For example, you are legally entitled to a break at regular intervals. Making a boundary that is supported by legal requirements is an excellent way to address some of your burnout without quitting your current job.

As mentioned in chapter 1, the exercises in this book also include physical activities or "rituals." Because your unconscious mind is unable to tell the difference between actions taken in symbolic form and those taken in real life, we can perform mini "rituals"—however silly they feel—to act out some of the psychological truths that we want to address in our lives. The key to creating a ritual is to set apart a special space and time for it. I like to light a candle at the start of a ritual and blow it out when the ritual is complete. Even taking a few deep breaths before doing the ritual can signal to your unconscious that you are doing something special.

RITUAL
Draw a Line

Sit on a paved driveway or sidewalk. After taking a few deep breaths and setting your intention to perform a ritual, use sidewalk chalk to draw a circle all the way around yourself. As you draw the circle, name the boundary that you are setting and maintaining. (For example, "I will not work through my lunch hour.") Then, take a second color of sidewalk chalk and trace over the circle, imagining yourself upholding that boundary in a scenario you expect to arise. Say the words out loud. ("Sorry, Bob, I can't make that meeting. I don't work through my lunch hour. Can we reschedule to later in the day?") If you feel like you need it, trace over the circle with a third color of chalk and envision yourself really standing firm, again saying the words out loud. ("I understand the urgency. I will have to watch the recording, as I'm unable to make it at that time.") This process can be repeated in concentric circles for additional boundaries.

The more boundaries you set, the more likely you are to get push-back from people in your life. You got to this place in your burnout process because their expectations were so high that you began a process of, as the WHO puts it, "chronic overwork." The next set of emotions you may have to deal with relate to disappointing others, especially if you are a people-pleaser.

People-pleasing habits and tendencies are encouraged by our society, and they are often positively rewarded in the workplace. People-pleasers can appear to be fantastic leaders and team players, but in reality, their actions are all about keeping themselves safe. A people-pleasing manager may be unable to say "no" to people in power about additional workload for their team. A people-pleasing coworker might overcommit to work projects or make promises to other team members that they can't keep. People-pleasing is often a root cause of burnout, and it is often a source for that inner-directed anger. By saying "yes" when we really feel "no," our insides respond with anger. A boundary has been violated. And that anger can easily become a form of insidious, brewing resentment.

Being able to say "no" when you mean "no" is vital not only for your own mental health and burnout recovery but also for the health of your team in your workplace. By courageously saying "no" when you are working at capacity, and not taking on more projects, you can help your manager hire more staff. (If you simply accept the overwork, the business will ignore their cries for help.) By courageously saying "no" to *unwritten* requests, such as the invisible demands of an "always available" company culture or an implicit expectation of participation in "voluntary" activities, you honor your boundaries and your anger. Yes, it feels like career suicide at some workplaces to say "no." It takes moral courage to say "no," especially to those in power above you. However, often this move not only helps you feel more at ease within your own self and body, but it garners respect.

Realistically, there can be repercussions for saying "no" to the wrong person or in the wrong way. This is how you found yourself in a place of burnout, after all. In this exercise, the idea is to brainstorm the ways to say "no" that won't get you fired.

EXERCISE
Upholding Boundaries

In your journal, dedicate a page for each boundary you outlined setting in the earlier exercises. Write that boundary at the top of the page. Now, imagine situations where you may have to say "no" to uphold that boundary. Write down three to five ways you might respond in that situation that don't include the word "no" itself. For example:

Boundary: I will not work through my lunch hour.

Scenario 1: Bob always books over my lunch. I swear he doesn't even look for availability when he slaps meetings on the calendar.

Potential ways I can say "no":

- "I'm unavailable at that time, but I notice we're both available at 2:30 p.m. Do you mind bumping it to then?"

- "I have a prior commitment at that time." (Bob doesn't need to know that the commitment is to go outside and get fresh air. That's none of his business.)

- "Yes! I definitely want to meet with you, and I'd love to schedule it for a different time so I can be fully prepared."

I once worked in a corporate job with an unwritten company culture that you couldn't say "no" at all, to anyone. In my role, I had to do just that. If I said "no" directly, they would either go over my head or stop asking me at all. A better way to approach this is to modify the improv-comedy rule of always responding to your scene partner with "yes, and. . . ." Instead, answer questions with "yes, if . . ." and include the specific requirements that need to take place to get to a "yes." When I was juggling too many projects, and I was asked to take another on, I could say "*Yes*, I'll take on this project, *if* stakeholders agree that I can deprioritize this other project." I once managed a person who agreed to a late-night website launch *if* she could take Fridays off those weeks. It's a great negotiation tactic that allows you to make clear what the trade-offs are between one thing and another. Sometimes the "if" conditions are impossible to meet, which means you then have grounds to say "no." You started with the word "yes," and they couldn't reasonably meet the needed requirements. If the requirements for the "yes, if . . ." can be met, then you have created a scenario of integrity, where your self-care and boundaries are maintained.

Because so much of the helplessness associated with burnout feels external to us and larger than life, one of the key activities at this stage is *discernment*. Just as we discerned where we have control or influence over situations (or not), we can also identify areas of our own personal power that we have given up over the course of becoming burned out.

EXERCISE
Identifying Personal Power

Using your "anger" list and your "boundary" list, create a list of six to eight elements of personal power that you have relinquished. Examples:

- I've given up my power to log off at the end of the workday.

- I've relinquished my ability to say "no" to my boss.

- I've given my partner the power to define our schedule on weekends.

If previous exercises haven't produced a usable list, try speed-writing several sentences that begin with the words "I've given up my power to _____" and see what bubbles up.

Use this exercise in the following ritual.

RITUAL
Take Your Power Back

Chop up some fruit, but only as much as you can eat during the ritual—about six to eight bites. I like apples, for their mythological significance, but any sort of sweet food would work. Set your space, lighting a candle and taking a few deep breaths. Move the plate of food away from you—just a little farther than arm's reach. Then name each piece of food with some element of your personal power that you have given up or given away in the process of becoming burned out. Then say out loud, "I'm reclaiming my _____." Reach out, stretch, and grab the piece of food that represents that piece of your power. Eat it slowly, considering how it feels to take that power back and what it will mean in your life. Repeat for each piece, being mindful of the stretch to grab it, the chewing and swallowing, and the intention and meaning of each piece.

You are going to disappoint others. Worse, you might disappoint yourself. Burnout recovery demands stepping back, slowing down, and taking some time to yourself. It demands breaks and peace. And you're going to have to navigate missing both internal and external expectations. If you're in the resentful, angry Fire stage of burnout, then letting down the team at work is not that hard to do, emotionally speaking. You've likely depersonalized and disconnected from the people and the work itself as a form of self-protection, making it easier to do just that.

EXERCISE
Expectations

Journal about the anxiety and sadness you feel, or any other feelings that bubble up, about disappointing other people in your life. Spend some time acknowledging your own expectations of yourself and how they are also affecting you. Take time to identify these emotions in your body—where do they sit, what do they feel like? How important are the expectations you have of yourself, or that others have of you, in the face of the need to recover from burnout?

Given that you probably can't quit your job, talking with your manager or supervisor is of utmost importance. Ask them to help you prioritize your tasks and make it clear that you cannot meet the same expectations as you have in the past. Ask for their help with either reassigning some of your work or getting things rolling to hire additional staff. In your one-on-one meetings with them (you should request these weekly if they aren't already on the books), go over your expected tasks, and tell them what you can realistically accomplish. Ask them which tasks should be left for later, which can be delegated to others, and which you absolutely must do. Repeat this process every single week. I know it feels tedious, but it's important. Your manager needs to be a part of your recovery, and by helping you prioritize and reducing your workload, they can be a powerful ally in this process. Often, I find that people who suffer burnout do so because (a) they don't want to disappoint their managers, or (b) their managers struggle to help them manage their workloads. This approach helps you "manage up" for these instances.

Note: Toxic workplaces are another matter entirely. I'm talking primarily about relatively healthy workplaces that simply have more work than they do people. Toxic workplaces will be covered more in chapter 4.

Burnout doesn't happen in isolation, however, so it's likely that you will also be disappointing family and friends as you say "no" to commitments with them. This is why *all* the people you live with are a part of your burnout-recovery support team. Sharing the mental and physical labor of running the household can go a long way toward reducing resentment, fatigue, and overwork. Many people are overworked at the office only to come home to a second job as "household project managers." Childcare, meal planning, housekeeping, parenting, caregiving, and emotional support for other people all count as additional work that can add to the stress of burnout. Openly discussing this workload in much the same way recommended above is a great way to begin to cut down on the expectations of your time, attention, and energy. This allows you to carve out some time to recuperate and recover.

EXERCISE
When Do You Say "Yes" When You Want to Say "No"?

In order to help guide some of the conversations you'll have with others around people-pleasing and the things you are saying "yes" to, you need to clearly understand what boundaries you are violating within yourself. This is another speed-writing exercise. As quickly as you can, answer the following questions:

1. What do I hate doing, but do it anyway?
2. Everybody always expects me to _____.
3. I resent it when I have to _____.
4. I never get to _____.
5. The last time I said "yes" when I wanted to say "no" was _____ and I felt _____.

Finally, the last person you are likely to disappoint when you stop people-pleasing is going to be yourself. If you have overachieving or type-A personality tendencies, then it's very likely that your expectations for yourself are far higher than those of your manager or your loved ones. It's important to get really clear on your own goals and priorities, in this case. Revisiting your objectives at work is a useful exercise for this. If you are doing work that doesn't relate to your specifically agreed-upon objectives, that's a "no," or at least a lower-priority task. If you are doing work that is outside your job description, that's also a "no," unless it comes with a raise and a new title. Businesses often promote people by asking them to take on more responsibility, so this rule doesn't have to be hard and fast as you grow in your career. But if you're burned out and serious about recovery, you have to clear your plate. You must do less—not more—work.

RITUAL
Setting Things Down

Often burning out is a case of carrying too heavy of a load and needing to set it down. Gather ten sticks or twigs, and after you set your ritual space by lighting a candle and taking a few deep breaths, name each stick with something you are setting down forever. (For example, "This is grabbing coffee for the team every morning," or, "This stick represents picking up other people's slack.") Bundle all ten of your sticks and carry them to the fireplace, the compost pile, or the trash can, and ceremoniously put them all down forever.

One of the things that firefighters can do in severe wildfire conditions is "contain" the fire. They can create containment lines to protect towns and homes by removing and reducing fuel sources for the fire, preventing it from passing through. Your boundaries are those containment lines. You have already set a few of them, but to truly get out of this phase, you will likely have to create even more. Containment lines have to completely encircle a wildfire, and no one is allowed to cross them. They are far firmer boundaries than you would normally expect in a healthy relationship with work or others.

Setting and maintaining boundaries will put you on the path to the next stage of burnout recovery; this is how to stop feeling like you're actively on fire and start healing. To a certain extent, these extra-firm boundaries are temporary, as is the reduced workload I've suggested in the exercises above. When we get to the Prevention phase of recovery, we will revisit these boundaries and see which ones need to stay in place and which ones can soften a little bit. However, to put out the fires of anger, you're going to need to say "no" a hell of a lot more than you usually do (even if it's just by declining meetings).

The Flood Stage of Burnout

Once you've mastered setting boundaries and reducing the sheer amount of work you're expected to do both at work and at home, and you've started letting some tasks simply not get done, you are likely to stop feeling so angry, resentful, and frustrated. At this point, many people will feel better for a while, but will then cycle right back around into burnout again. It is very common to skip the next step of burnout recovery because it's deeply uncomfortable. But you're brave, and you're committed to recovery. So let's talk about flooding.

EXERCISE
Floods of Feeling

In your journal, number a page from one to fifteen. Complete the sentence "I feel _____" fifteen times, as quickly as you can. Do any of your feelings surprise you? Write a longer entry about the discoveries this provides and consider discussing it with your mental-health provider.

There are two main emotions that rise with the Flood stage of burnout: fear and grief. The "fight" response of the sympathetic nervous system—anger—is empowering. It can fuel changes in behaviors and beliefs. Fear and grief are generally associated with "flight" and "freeze" responses. It's important to note that these are still sympathetic-nervous-system responses—you are still creating adrenaline and cortisol in this stage and are not at all out of the dangers of burnout. With wildfire, there's relief when the seasonal rains start, and the fires are extinguished by the thunderstorms. But that relief is temporary. Because now, there are no plants and roots in the forest to slow the flow of the water as it falls. Ruined soil and ash will not absorb it, and so it floods, carrying the debris and wreckage of the fire downstream with it. This wreckage, mudslides, and flash flooding are all dangers of the fire's aftermath.

RITUAL
Breathe

Through this stage of the process, it's a good idea to set reminder alarms on your phone to go off every hour or two. The notification should remind you to take three conscious, deep breaths. To tell the body that you're not in danger, focus on the inhale being about two or three counts shorter than the exhale. So: Inhale for four counts, hold for just a moment, and then exhale fully for six or seven counts. (It's okay to work your way up to this.) The parasympathetic nervous system, which helps us rest and recover, is triggered by the *exhale* part of the breath, which is why we focus on lengthening the outbreath. You can use this breathing technique any time you feel fearful or anxious.

If your "I feel" list in the previous exercise primarily showed feelings of fear, you're not alone. You are in the middle of the recovery process, the point where recovery feels impossible, and it's difficult to imagine how you'll feel on the other end. Sometimes, it becomes obvious to us that we have to make permanent changes in our lives—whether that is in our relationships, careers, work, or all the above. It can be more comfortable and easier to stay in the anger of the Fire stage than it can be to face these fears and deal with them directly. If anger is a signal that something needs to change and that boundaries have been crossed, then fear is an emotional tool used to guarantee survival. If you're experiencing a number of fears, it's likely that old childhood coping mechanisms are bubbling back up to the surface. The key here is gaining perspective. Your job is not a huge human-eating monster that will gobble you up. Having an outsized fight/flight response to an email at work is an experience of fear without perspective.

EXERCISE
Monsters in My Life

Craft, doodle, or cartoon several monsters or monster shapes. They don't have to be very artistic. Just be sure you make them look angry. Name each monster after things in your life that trigger outsized fear responses. Does one of them look like a Muppet in a necktie? Maybe that's the scathing department VP. Does one have big, sharp teeth? That one might be an unexpected bill. Now that you're lightening up about these things, write down how they can actually harm you. The vice president could fire you; the unexpected bill could wreck your credit score or cause you to incur extra interest on your credit card.

This is the crucial part! Now write about each of those scenarios in your journal in the following format: "If this happens, then I will _____." For example: "If the unexpected bill is impossible to pay, then I'll call the company and negotiate a payment plan, so it doesn't hurt my credit." Shifting unanswered "what-if" worries into "if-then" statements both shows you your own power in those situations and puts your fears into perspective. You can see which ones are manageable and relatively weak, and which fears truly have teeth.

It is likely that some of your fears are realistic and accurate, while others are outsized or unrealistic, based on childhood fears and the overwhelming state of stress you've been living in. There are two keys to managing this: first, using the breathing trick above to calm your stress response, and second, practicing discernment to understand which type of fear is which. It's a good idea to talk about childhood fears with your mental-health provider.

RITUAL
Discernment

Sifting through a ton of sensory and emotional inputs can be difficult and mentally taxing. In this ritual, we're going to set an intention to practice keen discernment and then sort something. It can be a jar of old buttons, a coffee can full of screws and nuts, or my favorite, the pieces of a jigsaw puzzle. In fairy tales, the heroes often have to do a chore of sifting or sorting small, fiddly items like seeds and lentils. Usually, they get help from birds or insects (representing the unconscious). By physically doing a discernment task, you are asking your unconscious for help.

The other big emotion associated with the Flood stage of burnout is grief. Grief can feel more exhausting and painful than anger, and it can be harder to process as a result. While anger feels empowering, grief makes us feel helpless and despairing. It feels like giving up. Water is associated with emotions and with tears, so the Flood stage of the burnout process may include deep wells of loss and sorrow. But flooding can also give us the ability to see the devastation caused by the fires in the harsh light of day. No one *wants* to grieve. But it is part of the path to recovery and part of the process of healing from burnout. While anger is an active emotion, grief is a more passive one. It requires a feeling of surrender, which many of us resist. It's common for people to job-hop or simply jump back into the Fire phase again to avoid this stage of recovery. The first step is to identify what you're grieving.

Grief can be described as "love with no place to go" or "letting go" or "loss." It is a form of sadness, a feeling of having had something we loved and enjoyed that is no longer available to us.

EXERCISE
Thinking About Loss

In your journal, write a list of five things that you have lost—that you used to love but can no longer enjoy or appreciate. Either talk with a member of your support team about these losses or write a journal entry about one of them.

RITUAL
Washing Away Grief

Because grief and flooding are so closely associated with water, this ritual is a water ritual. Even if you haven't taken a bath in years, draw a hot bath. Light a candle. And take a few deep breaths in the tub. While you're there, alone in the tub, let yourself fully feel your grief. It's okay to cry. It's okay to feel submerged by the sorrow. Let all of the things that you are grieving fall into the water. Envision this and hold it firmly in your mind. When you're ready, pull the plug to drain the tub, but don't get out yet! Feel, physically, the sensation of the water pulling away from your skin. Feel your legs get heavier as they no longer float in the water. Feel the sensation of letting go. When all the water has drained out, blow out your candle, and let it all go.

In the Flood stage of burnout, the damage has already been done. You are ready to leave a career behind and are daydreaming about "van-life" or homesteading. Many people tie large parts of our identities to our careers, particularly if we are very good at them. Some of those elements of your identity may be "burned up" in the process of your burnout. It's important to give yourself time to acknowledge and feel the losses associated with burnout.

The discernment ritual is important here, as well, because it can help you to discern what elements of your old life and your old way of being have been destroyed in the fire of your burnout. You will need to be very honest with yourself in this discernment process and pay close attention to the contents of your dreams. In my first burnout, one of the things that died was my enjoyment of data analysis. While I am still very good at it, I no longer found it fulfilling or pleasurable. It was no longer something I wanted to spend my workday doing. Because I was able to grieve that part of my skill set and focus my attention on growing my other abilities, I was better able to shape my work in ways that would meet my needs in the future.

Some people only need to grieve the loss of the satisfaction and achievement that they experienced prior to burnout, while many others may have to grieve the loss of entire portions of their identity. This identity loss can be very scary, and it is often tempting to stay in burnout rather than to pass through what psychologists call "ego-death." This process is a difficult and frightening one because the conscious part of our identity—called the *ego*—is afraid that it is literally dying. Ego-death is not actually life-threatening, but it can be pretty hard to traverse, because we are questioning long-held beliefs about self and identity. It's a good idea to have a mental-health professional available if you are going through such a loss of identity during this phase of change.

EXERCISE
Thinking About Identity

Make a mind-map of the things that make you "you"—from roles you play among family and friends to groups that you belong to or hobbies that you enjoy. Spend some time brainstorming this and even talk about it with loved ones.

RITUAL
Creating Identity

Create a piece of art that is a form of self-portrait. It can be a collage of magazine cutouts, a drawing, a painting, or a wire sculpture made of hardware from the garage. It doesn't have to look like anything or be worthy of hanging on the wall. What's important is lighting your candle and spending time intentionally thinking about who you are, creating something as a form of self-expression and self-depiction. Put this creation somewhere you can see it for the next few weeks.

The WHO only identifies burnout as it relates to the workplace, but the truth is that we don't work in a vacuum. We have friendships, relationships, and families outside of work that are also impacted by our burnout, if the fire blazes for too long. This may be due to our exhaustion and lack of availability for emotional connection; our misplaced anger and unhappiness; or our unhealthy choices to self-soothe, such as alcohol, substance abuse, or other forms of self-destructive coping.

After a wildfire, when the flames have been put out, the assessors move in and take stock of the damage done. Where is the soil still viable, and where is it burned completely? Where are the trees burned completely, and where might some of them return to life in the coming year? This damage-assessment process is an important one as you plan how to recover.

EXERCISE
Areas of Health

Draw a circle in your journal and divide it into eight equal parts. Number the pieces one through eight. With the center of the circle being "very unhealthy" and the outside edge of the circle being "very healthy," draw a dot in each sector of the circle to rate each of the following areas of your life:

1. Physical health (sleep, hydration, diet, exercise, regular healthcare)

2. Emotional health (self-expression, processing emotions, ability to name emotions)

3. Intellectual health (learning new things, curiosity)

4. Social health (spending time with friends, connection with community, sense of belonging)

5. Familial health (spending time with family, feeling supported by family)

6. Financial health (awareness of budget and spending habits, ability to meet financial goals)

7. Occupational health (feeling accomplishment and satisfaction at work, feeling appreciated for your work)

8. Spiritual health (feeling supported by something greater than oneself, feeling a sense of connection between oneself and others/nature)

It's likely that at this point in your burnout journey, the dot in your "occupational health" section is going to be located near the middle of the circle. However, it's also important to note that it's only one small part of the pie. Draw a line connecting the dots and look at your graph. If it were a wheel, could it roll? Where would it get stuck? Are there any areas of your health that you hadn't thought about recently, in terms of your overall well-being?

It is useful to repeat this exercise every six months or so, to see if there's an area of your wellness that has been forgotten or neglected. It can also help us to create healthier habits and self-care routines if we have an assessment of where we need the most help.

Talking to each member of your burnout-recovery support team is especially important during the Flood stage. This is usually their first opportunity to offer their observations and complaints about the repercussions of your burnout. Try to listen to their feedback without defensiveness and without rushing to create a solution. This is a time to sit with emotions.

If it's very hard to do this without feeling defensive, ask them to use the following format to speak their minds: "When you do _____, I feel _____." This format is very useful for having tough conversations that are deeply emotional. The best way for you to respond to someone who is making an effort to communicate this way is what's called "reflective listening." Your response would follow this format: "I hear you say that when I do _____, you feel _____." You can paraphrase a little bit, because the idea here is for them to feel *heard* and for you to ensure that you fully understand them. It's also a good idea for you to ask them to practice reflective listening as well when you're expressing your feelings.

EXERCISE
Inventory New Emotions

At this stage, it may feel like new ideas, projects, people, or emotions are coming at you almost too quickly to process—like a flood. Keep an inventory of these new emotions and circumstances throughout this stage. Journal or talk with someone about how you feel about them as they happen.

In the wildfire process, the rainy season passes, and though flooding remains an ongoing risk for several months, new life eventually begins to grow. This takes time and patience. Most of all, it requires rest. There are several different kinds of rest, and they don't all require you to be in your pajamas in bed—though that counts, too. Taking breaks from screens, reducing sensory input, and meditation are other forms of rest that might help your recovery.

Mental and emotional rest may mean getting some exercise or spending time outside. Our bodies self-regulate with sunlight. Getting some time outdoors can help regulate circadian rhythms, improving our sleep, mood, and feelings of well-being. I commit to playing an extended game of fetch outside every day with my dog. He loves it, and he is healthier, happier, and more well-behaved due to the exercise. It also gives me time outside, making me healthier, happier, and arguably more well-behaved, too!

Another form of rest is play. As adults, we often don't have time for recreation or think about it on a regular basis. But most hobbies are forms of play of one kind or another. Sure, games on our phones, video games, and board games all count as play. But if those things don't speak to you, you may have to get more creative.

EXERCISE
Rediscovering Play

Make a list of your top ten favorite things to do when you were six years old. What did you pretend to be? What toys did you play with? Which friends did you play with? Can you find a picture of your six-year-old self playing?

Make a list of your top ten favorite things to do when you were twelve years old. Who did you hang out with? What did you do for fun? Can you find a picture of your twelve-year-old self playing?

Now, make a list of how you currently play right now. If you have a Saturday afternoon alone in the house with no commitments, how do you spend it? What do you do for fun? Who would you hang out with?

Revisit those earlier lists; can you recapture any of those earlier forms of play? Maybe a fancy adult LEGO set would rekindle six-year-old you. Perhaps a bicycle would help you revisit that first taste of freedom from middle school.

Don't be alarmed if you sleep more during this phase. This phase of burnout recovery can look and feel a lot like depression. But grief is an exhausting emotion, and the Fire phase of burnout that you've just been through was also exhausting. If you are struggling to tell the difference between depression and grief, your mental-health provider on your recovery team should be able to help you.

The questionnaire most frequently used to screen for depression (the PHQ-9) is below. It's important to note that depression is an ongoing problem over several weeks or months, rather than a single moment in time. If you often, always, or almost always answer "yes" to the questions in the list below, then it's an indication of depression. If it's not all the time, or not consistent over time, it's more likely grief and burnout by itself. I recommend tracking your feelings for about six weeks. There are free phone apps that will remind you to ask yourself these questions and create a trend line of your answers over time. If you have persistent, ongoing indications of depression, then it's necessary to seek treatment and care.

If you have thoughts of self-harm, immediately call or text 988. Also, make an emergency appointment with your EAP counselor or mental-health provider.

Another common distinction between depression and burnout is that in burnout, often we can concentrate on things, have interests, and enjoy activities *outside of work*. When we feel "situationally depressed," that's indicative of burnout rather than depression.

Questionnaire: Modified PHQ-9 Depression Screening Tool[3]

Number a page from one to nine. Draw two columns. Label the first column "In General" and the second column "At Work." Now, rate each of the following questions on a scale of 0 to 5, with 0 meaning "never," 3 "sometimes," and 5 "always."

In the last two weeks, how often have you been bothered by the following problems?

1. Having little interest or pleasure in doing things

2. Feeling down, depressed, or hopeless

3. Having trouble falling or staying asleep, or sleeping too much

4. Feeling tired or having little energy

5. Having a poor appetite or overeating

6. Feeling bad about yourself—or that you are a failure or have let yourself or your family down

7. Trouble concentrating on things, such as reading the newspaper or watching TV

8. Moving or speaking so slowly that other people could have noticed—or the opposite, being so fidgety and restless that you have been moving around a lot more than usual

9. Having thoughts that you would be better off dead or of hurting yourself in some way

Total each column's numbers separately. Scoring:

- Above 27 in the "In General" column or in both columns: This may indicate a significant problem with depression. Please speak with your mental-health provider about this. Consider downloading an app to monitor the trend of these feelings over time.

- Below 26 in the "In General" column, but higher than 27 in the "At Work" column: This strongly indicates burnout, and not necessarily depression.

- Below 26 in both columns: This indicates that you do not have symptoms of depression.

The key to weathering the storms of the Flood phase is to rest and feel your feelings. Using your recovery journal as a safe place to express, explore, and vent feelings can be a healthy way to use this time. I strongly recommend using the health and well-being graph you created in the "Areas of Health" exercise earlier in this chapter to come up with an action plan for self-care. For example, if your physical-health score is low, set a modest sleep or hydration goal each day. This kind of gentle self-care will be helpful in later stages, and it might make it easier to rest and relax into the healing process. Self-care and self-soothing are your top priorities in this phase—as well as continuing to keep the fires out by upholding those firm boundaries from the earlier phase.

You will know you've reached the Regrowth phase when new ideas begin to sprout from your life's soil, when you begin to feel hopeful and joyful—even in the briefest moments. Because you've worked so much on feeling your feelings in the Flood stage, these moments of hope and joy should become as apparent in your journal as little baby plants germinating above the surface of the soil. You may notice that you sleep better at night, feel less exhausted during the day, and have more energy for regular activities or hobbies.

The Regrowth and Recovery Phase

Getting to the Regrowth phase of the burnout process is the point of this entire book. However, it is no faster or easier to achieve than the previous processes. With renewed energy, it can be easy to want to rush ahead. But that can lead to feelings of frustration and impatience when things don't come back to life as quickly as we want them to. After we have moved through the slow process of grieving and letting go in the Flood phase, new plants begin to grow in our burn scar. There are plants, like fireweed, that only germinate with fire. There are types of pines that are encouraged by fire to reproduce and seed. And there are some plants that grow in disturbed soil, that proliferate because of the damage that was wrought by the flames.

The thing to know about a burn scar is that it doesn't look like a forest anymore. Instead, the soil and burnt or fallen trees are covered in lots of little plants. Ideally, birds return to the area and bring with them new seeds. The regrowth of plant and animal life in a burned area is one of many little things, not big, towering trees and a canopy overhead. Here in New Mexico, groves of aspen trees in the burn scar were able to use their interconnected roots to survive during the Hermit's Peak/Calf Canyon wildfire, and they leafed out the very next spring.

Think about this metaphor in terms of your burnout: The big trees are gone. Large parts of your work, career, or identity that used to sustain you may be completely meaningless to you now. Grieving them is a part of the letting-go process. The trick is to look for the little things that are growing and sprouting instead. The emotions of this phase are subtle. They're not big, effusive feelings of joy—they're tiny seeds of curiosity and interest, glimmers and glimpses of possibility.

EXERCISE
Creating Your Forest

Draw (or paint, collage, or quilt) a forest representing your new life after burnout. This does not have to be an especially artistic rendering, but the more time you spend with it, the better. Colored pencils or markers may be very useful. Draw the big, burned trees that are probably not going to be able to be saved. It's up to you if you want to label them in your drawing, or just mentally note what they represent. Then draw in those trees and elements that might have survived the burn: the groves of aspens, or the really large, old trees that withstood the blaze. Finally, add the small insects, birds, and sprouting plants: the biodiversity that will encourage the forest to heal over time. You don't have to know what all of them represent. The act of drawing is one of inviting them in; their meaning will become more apparent to you in time.

RITUAL
Planting Seeds

In order to show your unconscious mind how seeds work, this ritual intentionally invites regrowth. Regardless of the time of year, lettuce seeds are able to be grown indoors. They are relatively easy to sprout, and they germinate pretty quickly. If you just can't stand lettuce, consider planting flowers, or you could even get a chia pet! The idea here is to consciously choose to plant seeds and to give them the warmth, moisture, sunlight, and patience that they require to sprout. Use a container out of the recycling bin and some dirt from outside, if you don't have seedling or potting soil. This doesn't have to be a production. The important part is the intention of growing something new and the metaphorical significance of watching it sprout and grow over time.

The burnout-recovery process often requires revisiting previous stages. Sometimes, we will go through the earlier steps in the process at a very rapid rate. You may have a day or two of feeling the burning anger rising all over again, then the grief and flooding, but in a matter of days (as opposed to the weeks or months it took before), you should be able to return to this phase of Regrowth. Just as flash floods can continue for months after a wildfire, your burnout emotions can return as well, but you now have more protection to weather any surprise storms.

EXERCISE
Revisiting Your Exercises

Now is the time to read back through your recovery journal and revisit earlier phases of your journey. What elements that led to your burnout are still a problem? What things are no longer a problem at all? How has your support team changed and developed over time? What does your wellness graph look like now?

RITUAL
Walking the Labyrinth

The road to recovery is seldom—if ever—a straight line. More often, it loops back on itself, and you sometimes seem to go backward before going forward. The labyrinth is an example of this kind of path, and it is a great metaphor for this journey. If there is an actual, physical labyrinth publicly available in your area, take the time to go walk it.[4] Start at the beginning, mentally asking yourself about your path ahead, and thinking about your burnout journey thus far. Pause when you reach the center of the labyrinth. Often, we will receive a new insight or idea in the center of the labyrinth. And then follow the path out—looping, backtracking, and circling around, thinking about how your recovery will probably be similarly circuitous. Be sure to write about the experience in your journal, as well as any "ah ha!" moments that may have occurred during or after your walk in the labyrinth.

It is 100 percent possible to recover from burnout without leaving your current job. It takes honesty and clarity with a manager who is willing to help you recover. It takes a relatively healthy workplace culture that can tolerate your new, healthier boundaries. And it takes the work you are doing to still feel interesting, useful, and meaningful.

Meaning is a tricky concept because it's very personal, and it's not often something we pay a lot of attention to in our daily lives. Meaning is often tied to personal values—another element of our lives that often goes unexplored and assumed. But now, you have a good opportunity to reassess your personal values and ensure they are in alignment with who you are, post-burnout, and who you want to be in the future.

EXERCISE
Discover and Rediscover Your Values

This is a mind-mapping exercise to discover your values—simply, a list of what is important to you. It's useful to have a couple of pens, markers, or colored pencils in a few different colors for this. You will be connecting and associating different ideas as you consider your responses to these questions.

- The most important people or relationships in my life are _____. It is important to me to be _____ with them. (Fill in the blanks here with positive adjectives, like *honest, loving, present, playful,* or *authentic.*)

- The three things I want to be remembered for in my obituary are _____.

- The person I admire most is _____, because _____. (The "because" indicates values!)

- The five most important things in life are _____.

Now, look at the connections, associations, and themes that emerge in your answers. I like to switch pen colors to draw circles around the themes that I see among the answers. For example, if I wrote that it was important to be authentic with my loved ones, and the people I admire most are "real and down to earth," that would be a theme. You might want to journal about these as your values, paying attention to how they have changed over time. For example, "hard work" used to be one of my values, but now, "satisfying work that makes a difference in peoples' lives" is my work-related value.

Values are hard to pin down, because they operate underneath our daily motivations and desires. They are also personal and unique to each of us. Other tools to help you identify your values include lists of values or quizzes available online, such as Scott Jeffrey's core values list (https://scottjeffrey.com/core-values-list) or the FranklinCovey "Mission Statement Builder," based on Stephen R. Covey's *The 7 Habits of Highly Effective People* (https://msb.franklincovey.com).[5] Values are personal, and identifying them is a personal process. The key here is to know what they mean for *you*.

Now, if you're still committed to staying in your current role, how can those values be applied to your existing job? This is a great conversation to have with your manager or someone from the human resources department. It may mean making a slight shift in your day-to-day tasks or having new objectives. But if your manager is partnered with you on this journey, they should be willing to look for ways to make this work. For example, if I want to do work that makes a difference in people's lives, then perhaps my role could shift to include mentoring others, rather than just being a daily grind of individual tasks. Having your work tasks align with your values can almost instantly make them feel less overwhelming and onerous. By ensuring that your daily workload is meaningful to you, you will be better able to stick it out through the recovery process.

Many people who experience burnout are in careers that are deeply rooted in personal meaning. People in "helping professions," such as physicians, therapists, nurses, teachers, and even clergy suffer some of the highest rates of burnout. This is because people in these jobs often see them as vocations—callings, if you will—which are very meaningful to them. However, meaning alone does not prevent burnout. You still have to say "no," practice firm boundaries, and maintain a lot of self-care even when the work is meaningful to you. Many of the people in these professions do not have the time to pursue hobbies, exercise, or create space outside of work, and it's often very difficult to take time off. Out-of-touch administrators and employers who don't support a healthy work-life balance or understand the deep emotional toll of the work often compound this issue.

This is where having a super-strong support system is important. Therapy, friendships, and family members that support you and create space for your emotional needs can be a lifeline. If they are voicing concerns about your looming burnout, it's a good idea to reflect on your boundaries (see exercises on pages 36–40) and feelings of personal power (page 41) in advance of burning out. Even if you're "just tired," consider their concerns as a reflection of how they perceive you moving through the world, and get yourself a little extra support.

With wildfires, sometimes embers lurk beneath the surface of the forest floor, only to erupt spectacularly a season later; these are called "sleeper" fires. Similarly, the "Fire" of burnout often happens behind the scenes when it comes to helping professions. These folks tend to show very little of the "Fire" of anger and jump right into the Flood stage of fear and grief due to loss of control, exhaustion, and frustration.

Because they are unable to address the "Fire" that is below the surface, they often cannot stay in the profession once they are burned out.

Many people—not just those in the helping professions—realize they need to make a major change when they reach the Regrowth stage. You might realize that your employer is not able to adjust to your new boundaries, or that your workplace is unable to help you shift into a more meaningful role. In this case, you may be able to stay in the same field but find a different place to work. Chapter 4 includes more exercises that can help you identify whether it's time to find a new workplace and how to prevent burnout in your new job.

Burnout can make getting away from your current workplace feel urgent. But if you decide it's time to change companies, try to be choosy and deliberate about it. It takes about six months to learn a new role, so you will be stressed out during that time, and more likely to slip back into old habits. Regardless of whether you're staying in the same field or switching careers entirely, being very honest with yourself in your journal or with trusted support-team members is vital.

EXERCISE
Checking In

When interviewing at a new company or turning in your notice, it's a good idea to check in with yourself on lots of levels. Here's a technique I use in my journal.

Head: Place your hand on your forehead. You are asking your frontal lobe to give its opinion on the matter. You want to know the logical pros and cons of the step you are taking, the rational reasons why this works or doesn't work for you. Write down two or three sentences based on your head's response. (The head is usually the part of yourself that you use in journaling, so this answer may be the most obvious and familiar.)

Heart: Place your hand over your heart. You are asking it for an emotional response to the issue. This response may not have a clear explanation, and that's okay. You just want to know your emotional truth. Write down two or three sentences that come to you when you ask your heart what its opinion is.

Gut: Place your hand on your belly. You are now asking your intuition to tell you what it thinks. This is a gut-level instinctual response, and I find is usually the most terse and to the point. Write two or three sentences about your gut's response.

Ideally, before making a major change in your job, relationships, or life, you want a consensus between your brain, heart, and gut. If you don't have consensus between them now, repeat the exercise and ask them each what they need to get to an agreement.

For some people who experience burnout, recovery may mean changing roles, industries, and even entire careers. The forest of your interests and abilities may have been devastated in the fire. In that case, you will need to do a little more self-discovery to figure out what you want to do next.

EXERCISE
Ikigai

The Japanese concept of *ikigai* has typically been understood in the West as meaning our best career or work. However, this is a mistranslation caused by different cultural values; in Japanese, *ikigai* itself is the *meaningfulness* that is ascribed to a person, relationship, or job.[6] (Think about your values mind-map earlier in this chapter.) However, the Western adaptation of the concept is useful for determining meaningful work. In this exercise, draw a Venn diagram with four circles that over-lap evenly. The four circles should be labeled:

1. What I'm good at

2. What the world needs

3. What I can get paid for

4. What I love doing

What you're looking for is the center—the intersection of all four of these circles. When I fill this out, I try to use verbs ending with -ing, so that I'm focused on activities rather than concepts. I might love "beauty"—and the world might need it, too—but "beauty" doesn't help me understand what a potential career might be. So I might put "writing," "creating," or "envisioning" instead of the more abstract concept of "beauty."

In the field of positive psychology, we recommend using one of your personal strengths every day. Like our values, personal strengths aren't always easy to pinpoint. There are several strengths assessments available online which can be very valuable in this regard, such as the HIGH5, VIA, and SSQ-72.[7] Assessing and knowing our strengths can be tricky, and they change over time. Even if you've done a strengths assessment prior to your burnout, it's a good idea to revisit this exercise now. Just as the once-deeply forested countryside is forever changed by wildfire, your strengths and interests may have shifted drastically in the process of burnout. You are a different kind of landscape now.

EXERCISE
Assessing Your Strengths

Make a list of ten times that you felt like you were "firing on all cylinders"—when you felt alive, successful, and high achieving, or when you were

doing something that you deeply enjoyed. Now, for each of those epi-
sodes, identify five to ten other things that you were doing at the same
time, using "-ing" words. You can also add these to your "ikigai" Venn
diagram, if they aren't there already.

As an example, one of my "firing on all cylinders" activities would be
writing a book about burnout. Things I was doing:

- Helping people

- Writing

- Researching

- Applying my expertise

- Brainstorming

- Listening to people

- Sharing unique perspectives

- Explaining complicated concepts in simple terms

You can use these lists to brainstorm new ideas for careers. Using
my example above, I may investigate whether I have the skills and cre-
dentials to write nonfiction books to help others.

After you've inventoried what you are good at, what you enjoy
doing, and what is meaningful to you, the next step is to find the jobs and
careers that use some, most, or all those aspects of who you are now.
If you're ready for a full career change, then skip ahead to chapter 4 for
more exercises to support that transition.

Sometimes the idea of a different job or career is overwhelming in
and of itself. This is where experimentation and play can be a fun way
to learn about those new, diverse little plants that are growing in your
new landscape. When little kids are playing with the idea of what they
want to be when they grow up, they sometimes dress up. One week,
they might wear a red plastic hat and imagine themselves as a fireman;

a week later it may be a hard hat or a cowboy hat. As adults looking for a new career, we can similarly imagine new roles as different "hats" to try on and swap around. Now that you've created your ikigai diagram and a list of potential new jobs, here are some low-pressure, beginner-friendly ways to explore a new path:

- Taking classes: This could include improv comedy, cooking, pottery—whatever idea gets you adjacent to one of the potential new jobs on your list. It might tap into a deep passion or simply be something you're curious about, or it might help you build skills that move you toward a career shift. After you've taken the class, consider how well it worked for you. Did it make you come alive?

- Volunteering: If you think that building houses will feel more meaningful and satisfying than being an accountant, then spend a weekend with Habitat for Humanity. Pay attention to how it feels to do the work as you do it. Do you like the spatial problem solving? The physical movement?

- Job shadowing: If you have someone in your network already doing something similar to the job you think you might want to do, ask them to let you shadow them for a day. This can give you an opportunity to ask practical questions about the work.

- Start a side hustle: Can you do the job on Fiverr or Upwork? Sure, you might make a few bucks, but the idea is to see whether it's fulfilling and something you can emotionally sustain.

In order to decide whether or not a new job or career is right for you, you have to first experience it in your body, feel the feelings that come up, and assess from there. Journaling before and after such experiments can be very useful.

With burnout, the urge is often to quit the job, the company, the industry, or the career completely, rather than to shift your existing role to find more meaning in it. Many people feel relieved by the idea of cobbling together a living via a series of pleasant side hustles during the Regrowth phase of burnout. Especially when the burnout-recovery process happens after a layoff, it's common to freelance, work odd jobs, and pick up part-time work for a time while exploring new career possibilities. The danger of doing that is that many hourly jobs can themselves lead back to burnout, especially part-time jobs that might seem low-stress at first, like food service or retail. Even in the case of layoffs, it's also not always possible to take time off if you don't have a spouse or partner who is able and willing to support you through this time. The most important parts of this process are to honor your limitations; explore new things that are growing inside you and activities that are meaningful to you; and try to align your work with your values.

Once the forest has grown back, and small trees and saplings are beginning to create habitat for more animals, then we move to the next stage, which is the prevention of any future fires. Like the Flood stage, the Regrowth stage requires patience and time. Regrowth doesn't happen overnight. But by focusing on what makes it meaningful and where your joy and energy is leading you, this process is likely to be more fun!

Preventing Future Fires

Starting a new job does not guarantee that you won't stay burned out, or that you won't burn out again rather quickly. Wildfire burn scars are at the highest risk of burning in the following fire season because they don't have the protective elements that the forest has. While starting a job with a different employer *can* make establishing and holding boundaries a little more straightforward or make it easier to set the standard for how much work you can accomplish in any given week, it doesn't change who you are or how you feel about the work itself. Even switching to a new career does not in itself protect you from burning out, as your passionate new interest, meaning, and joy can lead you to overcommit your energy.

EXERCISE
Defining Your Limits

Speed-write ten responses completing the sentence: "I got burned out because _____." Now look at those answers. Why did you get burned out? Was it people-pleasing? Bad boundaries? Toxic management? Toxic workplace? A combination of all the above? Now, boil those down to three or four things that you need to continue working on with your support team. Make a plan for each one, determining the accountability and support you will need, going forward.

   Example: I got burned out because I'm a people-pleaser and I have a hard time saying "no" when people ask me to do things. I'm going to work on this in therapy, particularly around my feelings about being and doing enough. I will also work on this at work and ask my manager to back me up when I need to say "no" or if I need them to say "no" on my behalf.

   By doing this self-examination and gathering support and accountability for the root causes of your burnout, you can prevent future fires effectively.

   The other thing that helps prevent future burnout is holding semi-regular check-ins with yourself. If daily or weekly journaling is not your jam, then set up a calendar block of one hour monthly to run through some of the exercises in this book. I recommend the speed-writing "I feel _____" set (page 32) and the "Areas of Health" graph (page 53) as regular check-in exercises, as well as the "Three Good Things" exercise from the beginning of this chapter.

   Chapter 5 also contains more information and tools to help prevent future burnout.

   Even with positive appraisals from a supervisor or peers, two things often get in the way of a sense of achievement: perfectionism and imposter syndrome. In fact, imposter syndrome is often a *cause* of burnout in several professions. To ensure a positive sense of achievement and to prevent future burnout, addressing imposter syndrome is an absolute must. Imposter syndrome is a feeling that you aren't "enough" for your current role—that you're underqualified, or that you "have everyone fooled" or "will be found out." Imposter syndrome usually comes from one of two states of mind: comparison with others or a sense of shame. When you're trying to identify and name feelings of shame, look for negative beliefs or statements that begin with the words "I am." Shame is tied to ideas of who we believe ourselves to permanently be. (As opposed to guilt, which is tied to "I did" statements about one-time acts.)

The truth is, the people who are truly imposters *don't feel imposter syndrome.* You must care about your work and commit to doing it well in order to feel imposter syndrome. Addressing this will help increase confidence, provide a sense of belonging at work, and give you a sense of accomplishment.

Diversity, Equity, Inclusion, and Belonging initiatives at many companies exist to help with feelings of imposter syndrome that might be rooted in historical inequalities. People from historically underrepresented races and classes often feel like imposters when working among coworkers who do not share their lived experiences of the world. Requesting a mentor at work who shares your background may be a great idea if this is the root cause of your feelings of imposter syndrome. There are also nonprofit organizations such as Empower Work (www .empowerwork.org) that offer support to workers in these situations.

EXERCISE
Imposter Syndrome

Create two columns, each numbered one through five. At the top of the first column, write "comparison," and at the top of the second column, write "shame." On a separate piece of paper, as quickly as you can, write down examples of situations where you feel like an imposter. Now, identify which of those statements are because you are comparing yourself to others. Look for the examples that include other people, such as "I always take longer than everyone else on the team to complete my tasks." Now, consider how you might reframe those statements by removing the other person. In the "comparison" column, rewrite them to reflect a more accurate depiction of yourself and your work. For example: "I am very careful not to make any mistakes in my work, which means I have fewer revisions to do later on. Though I take longer the first time, I don't have to go back later." If you struggle to rewrite the example, consider speaking with your support team.

The other statements might include the words "I am" in them. That is a flag that they might be about feelings of shame. A statement like "I'm not smart enough to be on this team" would be a "shame" example. Reframe those by making them either "I did" or "I do" statements, or really investigate the underlying beliefs that inform those feelings. Reframing the idea "I'm not smart enough" might pinpoint a specific instance rather than a broad generalization: for example, "I feel like I wasn't as prepared as I would prefer to be in Monday's meeting." By making it specific and tied to actions, you can now take steps to prevent feeling like that in the future—as opposed to a broad "I am" statement you can do nothing about. Alternatively, you might want to turn them into affirmations: "I am smart enough to be on this team, and I deserve a seat at this table."

Some of the most insidious forms of imposter syndrome involve both comparison and shame. "I'm not as buttoned-up as Patricia" contains both, and statements like this should be worked on in both columns. It is both a "shame" statement, because it's an "I am" statement, and a "comparison," because we're comparing ourselves to Patricia. So in the shame column, we would reframe that one to be more specific: "Patricia always has her notes ready before the meeting. I need to ask her how she gets the agenda items in advance, so I can prepare, too!" In the comparison column, we might reframe it this way: "I knew all of the key details in today's meeting, but I could have benefitted from a little more advanced notice of the agenda." There's a clear action here, and it's indicating a specific point in time rather than making a broad statement of comparison.

Once you have completed the columns, choose one of the items on your list and either write a journal entry about it or commit to discussing it with your support team.

Feelings of achievement and accomplishment are also next to impossible to experience if you're a perfectionist. Many people who suffer from burnout tend to give every single project they undertake far more attention and importance than it may warrant. It's common for our parents to have pushed for "straight A's," and far less frequent for us to have heard "C's get degrees." Perfectionism is most often rooted in feelings of fear. Whether it is an attempt to stave off unwanted criticism or prevent any possibility of failure, perfectionism is a refined, and often successful, way of dealing with sublimated fears. It is important to work with a mental-health professional about your personal causes of perfectionism to alleviate those specific fears. However, it's still possible to get a bit more comfortable with imperfection.

EXERCISE
Safety in Imperfection

Make a list of five projects that you have active right now that you wish to perform "perfectly." Now, prioritize those projects. One of them can be "A+" perfect. None of the rest can. Two more can be "B" work—not bad, but not perfect, either. The other three will then be "C" work— only adequate. That feels terrible and scary, doesn't it?

One of the easiest ways to prove to yourself that perfectionism is a waste of time and effort is to simply perform at a "B" or "C" level a few times and see that your work is still considered successful by your team and boss. But I know that's far more difficult to do than it sounds.

For the three "C" projects, speed-write four or five lines per project completing the phrase, "If it's not perfect, I'm afraid that _____." Assess those fears. Are they realistic? Are they likely repercussions for being less than perfect? If possible, see if you can right-size your fears to the actual likelihood of repercussion.

Now, how do you feel about applying the "80/20" rule to more of your low-priority projects? That is, if 20 percent of the work generates 80 percent of the result, where can you be less than perfect?

After wildfire, the landscape is permanently changed. Hiking in the Santa Fe National Forest, I can spot ancient burn scars that have recovered fully, yet are deeply different from the rest of the forest that surrounds them. The key to recovering fully from burnout is to pass through all the phases of recovery and not get stuck in a constant cycle of burn-exhaustion-burn. Once you've been down this path, you may find that you're asked to be on someone else's burnout support team in the future.

If, however, your professional burnout seems to extend its fingers into other areas of your life—impacting sensory sensitivities, food preferences, and energy levels—it's possible that you are experiencing a different, more profound kind of burnout related to being neurodivergent.

CHAPTER 3

Applying the Wildfire Metaphor to Neurodivergent Burnout

THE TERM "BURNOUT" may have more complicated meanings for neurodivergent people. Even if you do not consider yourself neurodivergent at all, your symptoms of burnout may extend beyond those described in chapter 2; you may have completed all of the exercises and rituals and still have burnout symptoms that are raging out of control. Neurodivergence is a growing field of study, and new diagnostic criteria are still being formed. Many older adults are now realizing, often only after severe burnout, that they may be neurodivergent. The exercises and tips in this chapter may be of value regardless of whether you have been formally diagnosed with any form of neurodivergence.

It's possible that you already know about and understand your neurodivergence, and you are seeking help with recovering from the devastating loss of skills and coping tools that come with neurodivergent burnout. If that's the case, and you skipped directly to this chapter, I'd like to recommend that you look at the exercises and tools outlined in chapter 2 before tackling this section. Many people suffer from both professional and neurodivergent burnout simultaneously. Further, many of the exercises, rituals, and tactics in chapter 2 lay the groundwork for those found in this chapter.

The wildfire metaphor can be applied to the neurodivergent burn-out process as well as the professional one. Unfortunately, the "wild-fires" of neurodivergent burnout are often more destructive and frequently cause more permanent damage. Again, I'd remind readers that this process is more of a spiral than it is a pure circle—you will be looping back to previous stages again and again through the process of recovery. Don't get discouraged if you discover you are earlier in the process than you originally thought.

In order to understand what actions are needed right now, it's a good idea to assess (a) whether your symptoms are consistent with neurodivergent forms of burnout and (b) where you are in the burnout process, as it pertains to possible neurodivergence. I should note that neurodivergent burnout is an area of ongoing research and does not have a lot of supporting evidence in peer-reviewed publications. Adult experiences of neurodivergence have escaped scholarly and medical notice for many years, and many descriptions of neurodivergent burn-out and tactics for recovery are based on the anecdotal and experien-tial data of adults who have been through it ourselves, like me.

Questionnaire: Assessing Neurodivergent Burnout

For each item, score how true each statement is for you *right now*, with 1 being not at all true, and 5 being very true.

- Sounds that I used to be able to ignore bother me a lot these days.

- I have to turn off the lights when the world gets too loud.

- My dietary choices are more restricted than ever.

- I can't socialize like I used to.

- I spend a lot of time resting alone in the dark.

- My pets, family, and loved ones irritate me far more than usual.

- I feel like I've lost IQ points.

- Work that used to be easy doesn't come easily anymore.

- My rage erupts out of nowhere.

- I have an extremely short fuse.

- Sometimes it's hard to verbalize my thoughts or feelings at all.

- Sometimes I can't stop verbalizing everything that goes through my mind.

- I can no longer tolerate scented candles or perfume around me.

- I can't handle the same stress levels I used to maintain with ease.

- I know I need to do things, but I can't force myself to start.

- I feel overwhelmed all the time.

- I feel like I'm lazy and procrastinating.

- I have frequent anxiety attacks (or panic attacks).

- My senses feel like they have the volume turned all the way up.

- I don't feel like I can "play the game" of politics with people anymore.

Scoring: Add your numbers together to determine your likely stage.

- If you scored between 20 and 35: This means you are most likely in the Regrowth or Prevention stage of burnout. You may recognize earlier stages of your burnout experience in a number of the above statements. The recent appearance of some of these elements might mean you should take immediate action to prevent further problems.

- If you scored between 36 and 65: This is likely the Flood stage, though this is an unclear middle ground. It's going to take a few more exercises to identify where you were before and where you feel like you're heading.

- If you scored over 66: This indicates that you are most likely in the Fire stage of burnout. This is the most devastating stage and can often be full of surprises and frustration.

In the next several sections, we will cover in depth what each stage feels like and what you can do to process, heal, and recover from neurodivergent burnout. As mentioned above, this chapter *builds* on the information in chapter 2. It's possible to use both chapters concurrently if you are experiencing professional and neurodivergent burnout at the same time.

I use "neurodivergent" as an umbrella term in this chapter, unless I'm specifically referring to a particular form of neurodivergence. This umbrella term includes autism, ADHD (Attention-Deficit/Hyperactivity Disorder), and the combination of the two (often called AuDHD), as well as dyslexia, Tourette's syndrome, apraxia, dyspraxia, OCD, synesthesia, and epilepsy, among other conditions. My personal experience is with autistic burnout, so examples may lean in that direction more than others. However, because neurodivergence is the experience of living in a world that is often uncomfortable, unyielding, and frustrating, I believe many elements of burnout carry across various types of neurodivergence. While there is almost no literature on adult autistic burnout, there is even less about the other forms of neurodivergence and their experience of burnout. Some symptoms of neurodivergent burnout like long-term skill regression and heightened sensitivity may be autism-specific, but given the fact that these are the result of long-term taxing of systems, I doubt it. It bears much further research.

While typical burnout symptoms include exhaustion, overwhelm, skill regression, and loss of coping skills, each of the stages has other underlying feelings as well.

- The Fire stage is dominated by ANGER. You may experience impaired executive function at this stage, and meltdowns and shutdowns may become more frequent.
- The Flood stage is dominated by GRIEF. Expressing emotions and establishing routine are key activities for this stage, as well as ongoing work to address sensory overload.

- The Recovery stage is dominated by CURIOSITY, NEW JOY, and possibly even HOPE. You may find your special interests changing, or you might discover new ones.
- The Prevention stage is dominated by DETERMINATION or STRENGTH. Practicing self-care, acknowledging support needs, and creating an "early-warning system" are all necessary to prevent future experiences of neurodivergent burnout.

Working with emotions can be especially tricky in a neurodivergent context. Many neurodivergent people, especially those with autism or CPTSD (complex post-traumatic stress disorder), also have a condition called *alexithymia*, which is an inability to name or express emotional states.[1] The journaling prompts and exercises in this chapter are designed to circumvent this, and they may even help with overcoming alexithymia in the long term.

In my own experience of alexithymia, learning about emotional states could be compared to learning about colors in elementary school. We are first taught the primary colors—blue, red, and yellow. Then the secondary ones—green, orange, and purple. Over time, we might be given a 164-color crayon pack or learn how to mix paints to make more nuanced colors. Similarly, we need to first learn about our primary emotional states before we can identify more complex ones. As identified by psychologist Robert Plutchik, the basic human emotions are:

Anger	Anticipation
Sadness	Trust
Joy	Surprise
Fear	Disgust

When you get stuck with identifying an emotion, you can use this list to help you pinpoint what you are feeling. Try to use the list like a multiple-choice question, where you have to select one of the answers. When I started this process of learning to name my emotions, my list was limited to just four feelings: mad, sad, glad, and afraid. (The rhyming scheme helped me remember them.) After several months of using this short-ened list, I then worked on adding the remaining basic emotions. At first, choosing from a list of just eight emotions can feel like a relief. It simplifies the answer to the question of what we're feeling. However, over time, the "primary color" feelings start to seem insufficient—we're missing hues and shades. For example, when trying to understand the emotion of "lone-liness," I started by thinking of it as a *shade* of sadness. This is an inexact practice, and there is no perfect way to do it. In the exercises that follow, you can still get what you need out of them just by choosing from the list of the basic emotions. If you'd like to expand your emotional vocabulary, there are multiple "color wheels" of human emotions available online.[2]

Like professional burnout, neurodivergent burnout requires a sup-port team to help you through the recovery process. Remember, no one fights a wildfire alone! As mentioned in chapter 2, it's important to assemble your team early and make sure to have regular check-ins with them. We've covered this already in chapter 2, but your burnout-recovery support team should include:

- Someone who can understand your emotions, reflect them back to you, and validate your experience—preferably without rush-ing to offer solutions. (This is where an EAP counselor or ther-apist is useful.) It's important that this person is informed about neurodivergence and complex trauma.

- Someone who can help you have fun and play. Friends, kids, and pets are great for this. Lean on these team members to get exercise, enjoy the sunshine, and take breaks.

- Someone who can help you prioritize tasks and reduce the amount of stuff that's expected of you. Managers and spouses both fall into this category. By being honest about your burn-out and asking for help, you can often find ways to reduce your overall workload. This can help you create more time for your-self and your recovery.

Neurodivergent burnout requires more support for recovery than professional burnout, because it relates to your whole existence rather than just your workplace. Because of this, your neurodivergent-burnout recovery team should also include:

- Everyone sharing your living space. Because environmental factors can exacerbate burnout, it's important that absolutely *everyone* in the household is on board with your recovery process and plan.

- Someone close to you who does *not* share your living space. It is important to have someone on your team who can take a more neutral position than someone you are living with. This should nevertheless be a person who can understand and validate what you are going through. Social media can be a good resource for finding this support-team member.

Here are a few definitions for terms commonly used within the adult autistic community.

Meltdown: *A meltdown is an uncontrollable eruption of extreme emotion and distress due to overwhelm. It is often misinterpreted by others as a "tantrum"—but while a tantrum can be stopped, a meltdown cannot.*

Shutdown: *Shutdown also is an extreme emotional response to overwhelm, but it is directed inward instead of outward. Sometimes, shutdowns happen after meltdowns. It is typified by a reduced ability to speak, stay awake, or interact with others.*

Special interests: *Whether they are activities or topics, special interests provide stress-reducing effects, such as slowing breathing and lowering blood pressure. Spending time with special interests is important for stress management.*

Stimming/stims: *Stimming is any activity that helps a person release excess energy, excitement, or emotion. Hand-flapping and* *rocking are common and recognizable stims, but many people stim in more subtle ways, including clicking their tongue, rubbing their feet together (also known as "cricket feet"), enjoying scented candles, or playing musical instruments. Some people may use fidget toys or other "stim tools" like silicone chew necklaces.*

Samefoods/safe foods: *These are consistent foods that can be eaten without sensory distress.*

Executive function: *Many neurodivergent people have impaired executive function, which is the ability to prioritize, start, or complete tasks—even if they want to do them. This often includes housekeeping and daily hygiene tasks.*

Masking: *When neurodivergent people have to consciously choose to "act" neurotypical in order to navigate complex social situations, it is called masking. Masking might include suppressing tics or stims, making uncomfortable eye contact, or putting on a persona for the comfort of others. Masking is very common in late-diagnosed and undiagnosed adults.*

As in chapter 2, I recommend having a dedicated journal or notebook as you work through the exercises in this chapter. This journal should be kept private from other household and support-team members. Additionally, I strongly recommend the following tools to support you through your recovery journey:

- Nourishing safe foods/samefoods: When under extreme stress, foods can be a source of sensory overwhelm. Lean into your "samefoods" during this time, guilt-free. (I lived on protein shakes, gluten-free chicken nuggets, and cheese for months during my burnout recovery).
- Sensory comfort items: While some sensory triggers are upsetting and overwhelming, it can be soothing and healing to discover sensations that bring you relaxation, comfort, or delight.

For example, I like candlelight, very soft sensations, and certain kinds of music.

- Stim tools and toys: Anything you like to use to siphon off extra physical and emotional energy will be helpful through this process. Fidget spinners, musical instruments—the list is endless.
- Sensory protection: If you haven't invested in noise-canceling headphones or filtering earplugs, now's the time. Sunglasses, ear protection, and other forms of sensory protection can help ease the stress on your senses while you work on recovery.
- Special-interest items: Surround yourself with things that remind you of your special interests during this process.

These tools will be used in some of the exercises to follow, but they are also helpful on their own to create the mental and emotional space you need at this time. They are intended to create a sense of safety and a little bit of emotional "padding" to make the work of recovery possible.

In the Raging Inferno of Neurodivergent Burnout

The overarching emotional state that is associated with the Fire stage of burnout is *anger*. To put a point on it, just existing in the world can give neurodivergent people a whole lot to be angry about. However, the specific causes and sources of the anger can often be hidden. Depending on other factors in your life—such as complex trauma or family dynamics, as well as alexithymia—you may not even recognize what you're feeling as anger. We often internalize and bottle up our anger, until it explodes out of us in the form of a meltdown or implodes, causing shutdown.

Meltdowns, shutdowns, and anger are not the causes of burnout in and of themselves. In isolation, each of these things is a way your brain is trying to help you cope with overwhelm. However, when they happen one after the other, or they feel like a constant state of being rather than a temporary coping mechanism, then we're in the blazing inferno of the Fire stage. Rather than trying to suppress or ignore meltdowns, shutdowns, and anger, it's more useful to see them as signs of larger, underlying problems. The exercises and activities in this section will help you uncover the root causes of your burnout, rather than treating anger or meltdowns as "bad" or "shameful." They are important sources of information; your body and mind are telling you something. The trick is knowing how to translate that information into something useful.

EXERCISE
Meltdown Analysis

This is not a one-time assignment: You will be adding to and revisiting this exercise throughout your recovery process. Each time you experience a panic attack, meltdown, or shutdown, repeat this exercise. For this first time, consider your most recent meltdown/shutdown experience. Take a deep breath, and then write down a timeline and description of the event and the things leading up to it. Write down anything you notice about it as you remember the situation.

Now, answer the following questions as quickly as you can—don't spend more than five seconds thinking about each one!

1. Where do you feel sensations in your body as you remember the event? Do you remember any physical sensations during the event itself?

2. Can you identify what caused the event? For example, this could be specific sensory triggers, a combination of things over time, etc. List the specific triggers.

3. Go back to the basic human emotions list (page 81). Which one of these was the primary emotion you felt before the event? Which

one did you feel during it? Did that emotion change after it was over? (Choose only ONE emotion to answer each question!)

4. Take another deep breath and think again about the timeline of the event. What was the earliest warning sign in your body, mind, or behavior that you were headed into a meltdown or shutdown?

This exercise, repeated every time you have a meltdown, shutdown, or panic attack, provides vital information for your recovery from burnout—and for your own self-understanding. Having repeated this analysis of my own meltdowns over several years, I now notice earlier and earlier warning signs. For example, I now know that if I'm feeling frustrated or impatient with my household pets, that's an early sign of an impending meltdown. I then take some time alone in a dark, quiet room and reduce my level of overwhelm preemptively, which often heads off the full-blown event.

I also find when I do this exercise that my list of emotional states almost always includes anger. Often, it's bottled-up anger (due to overwhelm, sensory discomfort, boundary violations, or frustration with myself) that causes the meltdown in the first place. I sometimes feel and express anger at myself and others during the event (for example, yelling at my pets). And though my primary post-meltdown feeling is usually sadness or shame, it can sometimes also be anger about the circumstances that led up to the event.

As we explored in chapter 2, anger emerges when we sense that a violation has occurred; it's a signal that *something needs to change*, and it provides energy to create that change. If we do nothing about it— bottling it up—that energy builds inside us. In chapter 2, I discussed how in a professional, neurotypical context, this is typically due to boundary violations. In a neurodivergent context, it can additionally be caused by sensory triggers, by stress and overwhelm, by perceived injustices, and by demands that feel autocratic or unreasonable. The first step to working with our anger as a tool, rather than seeing it as a problem, is to know when we can use that energy safely to affect change in our lives.

When I was a kid, my mom used to recite the "Serenity Prayer" to me frequently. This was because I was an overwhelmed autistic kid who was angry about so much, so often. What's important about this prayer isn't appealing to a deity (unless that is part of your belief system). It's what the prayer is seeking: the courage to change what we can, the strength to accept what we can't change, and the wisdom to know the difference.

EXERCISE
Things I Can Change

Make two columns on a page of your journal. At the top of one column, write "Things I Can Change" and at the top of the other, "Things I Can't Change." You're going to practice your "wisdom" in this exercise. Think about your most common sensory triggers, the things that most frequently make you angry, or typical causes of meltdowns and shutdowns. Now decide which of the two columns each thing belongs in, and write it down. Some sensory triggers can be controlled: I can wear ear protection or earplugs in a loud space. Others are harder to change: I live under a flight path of a nearby airport, and the planes flying overhead bother me. Unless I'm able to move, this would go in the "Things I Can't Change" column.

Now, on the next page of your journal, make a list of the things you can do to address those problems written in the "Things I Can Change" column. Commit to doing one of them today (and another one next week, and another the week after that). When you feel angry about anything in this column, use that anger as energetic fuel to do something about it.

The items that are listed in the "Things I Can't Change" column are harder to deal with, because you have the rocket-fuel of anger but no way of using it. In this exercise, you've already used your own wisdom to discern which items go in each column. Now, I recommend getting additional wisdom from members of your support team: Talk it through with them, and see if any items could shift into the "Things I Can Change" column. If not, are there any other, adjacent sensory triggers that you can control?

For example, the high winds in the springtime in New Mexico are very loud. They have no rhythm, and they make my dog extra clingy, as wind fills him with anxiety. The sound of the winds themselves is overstimulating to me, and short of wearing ear protection 24/7 in my home, they are inescapable. They are in my "Things I Can't Change" column. So I find other sensations I can control: I turn on fewer lights. I only eat samefoods. I wear softer clothing. These sensory concessions reduce other forms of sensory overwhelm, making it just a little easier to deal with the sensory discomfort of the winds.

By feeling and acknowledging your anger, identifying its sources, and then determining what can be done about it, you allow the anger to flow through and out of your body. This alone can prevent meltdowns or panic attacks and tamp down some of the flames that lead to burnout. Discussing these things with your support team also allows you to "vent" some of that anger in a constructive way.

I've mentioned "panic attacks" alongside meltdowns and shutdowns because it's possible they aren't panic attacks at all. For many late-diagnosed or undiagnosed neurodivergent adults, the experience of what we call "panic attacks" are in fact meltdowns. While both panic attacks and meltdowns are uncontrollable, can cause chest tightness, and often include tears, panic attacks also include numbness in the extremities and face due to lack of breathing. Meltdowns will include sensory overwhelm, such as sensitivity to sound or light. Of course, it's entirely possible for a person to suffer from both. Understanding triggers, noticing early warning signs, and discerning emotional causes are useful activities for both meltdowns and panic attacks. Further, frequent occurrences of either kind of event are a sign of impending or active burnout.

Earlier in this chapter, I suggested gathering tools that can bring you comfort, such as your "samefoods" or favorite stim toys. This is because working through a book like this can be triggering, and if you're actively in a state of burnout, it's likely that you're already teetering on the edge of a meltdown. By leaning into those things that provide solace and comfort, you will be able to support yourself through the discomfort that might come up while doing the exercises. If you haven't already identified what those comfort items and activities are for you, this next tool will help.

EXERCISE
Make a Self-Care Menu

Do this exercise when you're feeling good. I strongly recommend being as silly and playful as you can with this one—you're making something that you will enjoy seeing and using. Create a poster or card with a restaurant-style menu. Make different sections for appetizers, entrées, and so on. Now brainstorm things that you can do to make yourself feel better when you're feeling overwhelmed and in need of care. The purpose of this menu is to give your future self a break when you get overwhelmed; you won't have to think of what you need, because you'll already have it written down.

Doing this ritual at a time when you're feeling good will help make sure it's a solid list. Feel free to ask your support team or search online for ideas as well, but make sure that your list is personalized to your specific preferences. Some typical self-care menu items are:

- Drink a glass of water

- Eat something with protein

- Stand in the sun for ten to fifteen minutes

- Take a shower

- Spend time with my special interest

  I like to include some of my favorite physical activities as well:

- Solo dance party!

- Swing on the swing

- Go for a walk

- Sing

Use your self-care menu as often as needed. I recommend pinning it to a wall or somewhere you can easily see it when you're struggling. (I often forget mine exists when I'm having a bad day.) You will most likely be reworking this or adding to it over time, so don't worry if it's not perfect.

In my list of self-care menu ideas above, you'll notice that I included physical activities or sensations that help me to self-regulate. The common term for this kind of activity is a stim or stimming. While stimming is often associated with autism, you don't have to be autistic to benefit from it or use it as a form of self-care. Further, evidence suggests that proactive or prophylactic stimming can help with long-term self-regulation of emotions and physical energy.[3] The most well-known form of stimming is hand-flapping or rocking (a stereotypical trait often seen in television depictions of autistic people), but that's just the tip of the iceberg of the vast world of stims.[4]

Each of our sensory areas can be overwhelmed or triggered negatively, but they can also each be stimulated in a way that is soothing or energizing. The chart below shows examples of possible triggers or possible stims for each of the eight sensory areas. Yes, eight. You're probably familiar with the five senses—sound, smell, sight, touch, and taste. The three additional ones are:

- Interoception: The sensation of internal bodily states such as having to urinate, hunger, or thirst. Impaired interoception can lead to eating disorders, late bed-wetting, and an inability to respond to temperature changes or pain.

- Proprioception: The sensation of where the body is in space, affecting how we hold our body in posture and alignment. Proprioception is tied to the vestibular system and balance. Holding our hands loosely raised in front of us—often called "T-Rex arms"—is a common way of self-soothing when we aren't paying attention to proprioception.

- Kinesthetic awareness: The sensation of how our body moves. This awareness is heightened in athletes and dancers, and it can be a form of stimmy play for many people.

The list of sensory triggers and stims below is in no way comprehensive. It's going to be highly personal for each individual. You may want to make a chart like this in your journal with your own, personal versions of these things.

SENSORY SYSTEM	STIM EXAMPLES	TRIGGER EXAMPLES
Sound	ASMR videos[25] Soft, rhythmic sounds Loud music (often familiar)	People eating Loud, unexpected sounds High-pitched noises and beeps
Smell	Naturally scented candles Fresh flowers	Artificial air freshener Detergent

SENSORY SYSTEM	STIM EXAMPLES	TRIGGER EXAMPLES
Sight	Bright, supersaturated colors Amber lights, candlelight Sparkly, glittery things	Bright fluorescent or blue-toned lights Busy, distracting scenes or patterns
Touch	The soft fur of a cat Soft clothing with no tags	Itchy tags or seams on clothing Microfiber
Taste	Strong or very spicy flavors New foods	Unexpected flavors Foods that vary in consistency
Interoception	Masturbation, sexual stimulation Mouth/tongue movements Compression	Constipation Pain Menstruation
Proprioception	Swinging or rocking Ecstatic dance, twirling	Heights Claustrophobia
Kinesthetic	Going for a walk, run, or bike ride Tai chi, yoga, or similar mind-body activities	Forced, mindless stillness (for example, at a school desk or office)

A chart like this can help inform which items you put on your self-care menu. It can also help you create a list of triggers to potentially avoid when stress is running high. If you are under a great deal of stress from any source, limiting and reducing things on your "triggers" list and increasing things on your "stims" list can help with self-regulation and stress reduction.

Physical exercise and movement are particularly useful at this stage of the process. Linear movements such as walking, running, and cycling are the most soothing for most bodies and neurotypes. It can be helpful, too, to get time outside in the sunshine for emotional regulation.

RITUAL
Walking Meditation

I recommend walking daily for about twenty minutes, if you are able. If you don't like walking, or get easily bored or distracted try some of these exercises while you walk:

- Mentally catalogue your sensory experiences—the things you see, hear, touch, taste, or smell.

- Take a phone or camera with you, and take at least five photos of things that catch your eye. You can choose a color or type of thing you want to photograph and look out for it, such as "orange things," "satisfying things," or "things that are ugly but compelling."

- Listen to music or talk with a friend while you walk. (There's nothing saying you must do this by yourself!)

Whatever you end up doing, remember that the walking itself—and building a routine around it—is the important part.

Something that can cause a great deal of anger—and a lot of meltdowns—for neurodivergent people is called "PDA." This acronym stands for "Pathological Demand Avoidance," a term that many folks feel stigmatizes a relatively common experience. (In recent years, the online community has been "rebranding" PDA as "Pervasive Drive for Autonomy.") At its most basic level, PDA means that anything that is perceived as a demand is immediately and vehemently rejected. This response is particularly strong when the demands feel unreasonable or nonsensical—which happens all the time in a world that does not bother to explain "why" it is demanding what it demands.

You might have seen a video on social media that demonstrates what PDA might look like in action: A person with a PDA profile sees a household task that needs to be done, such as washing dishes, and they take the initiative to do it on their own. A parent or partner wanders by and asks, "Hey, can you wash the dishes?" At this, the person immediately stops washing the dishes, in the middle of wiping a sudsy skillet. Because it was asked of them, it now feels like a *demand*. This is a relatable experience for many of us; sometimes we can grit our teeth and finish washing the skillet (or whatever we're doing), but often the overwhelming urge to resist a request is enough to make us stop. It's very frustrating to parent or partner a person like this, and most of the literature surrounding PDA focuses on that experience. However, speaking as a person who has this neurological quirk, it is an *ongoing* source of frustration and anger for us—not just temporary or situational— and it can cause or exacerbate burnout.

Here's another, relatively harmless example: I get irrationally angry when my dog asks to go outside right after we've come back home. Even though I know that it's best to take him outside when he asks, both for him and for me (so that I can avoid cleaning up any accidents or paying additional vet bills), I don't want to do it. The more he breathes on me—staring into my soul with this *demand* to go outside— the less willing I am to take him. I know that I should and will eventually take him outside; I just need him to relax and leave me alone for a few moments to collect myself. Dogs, however, do not comprehend this. This exchange infuriates me, causing me to feel a lot of anger and frustration, both with the dog and with myself. However, PDA-related anger does usually go in the column of "Things I Can Change." In this situation, I can go to another room, shutting the door and leaving him outside of it. I give myself two or three minutes to breathe and take a break away from his demand. After that, I'm able to immediately take him out without re-triggering the stubborn refusal to do what had been asked of me. Counting to ten sometimes works, too.

Another way to address PDA-related feelings of anger is to discuss with your support team how they might change the way they make "demands" of you. Communicating "demands" differently can short-circuit the PDA process, reducing your experience of stress and anger. One way to do this is to reframe demands as solving a problem. Rather than asking you to do a specific thing, they can state a problem and ask for your help. This circumvents the demand and instead gives you a chance to offer your assistance. Instead of asking, "Can you do the dishes?" a support-team member may say, "Wow, this kitchen is really overwhelming right now. It's stressing me out. Is it stressing you out? How can we fix it?" You may not want to do the dishes; maybe the sensory experience of hot, soapy water is too much for you right now, making the question "Can you do the dishes?" feel like a frustrating boundary violation. Changing the request to a more open question allows you to offer to help in other ways, like taking out the trash or scrubbing down the countertops. Yes, the other person now has to do the dishes themselves—but cleaning up the kitchen has become a cooperative exercise rather than an infuriating battle of wills. While your support-team members may not immediately change their way of communicating with you, if they see its effectiveness, they might learn to adjust! Especially when the result is more cooperation and less stress or anger on your part.

In chapter 2, we explored the connection between an anger response and boundary violations. This is a critical assessment for neurodivergent folks to carry out, as well. Sensory issues can indeed feel like boundary violations, as can the demands that trigger a PDA response. These are often unspoken boundaries: For example, "I can't handle loud noises right now; please don't make them." Frequently, you may not even be aware that those boundaries exist until they are crossed. This is why an important part of your burnout-recovery process is discovering your own boundaries and sharing them with your support team. Setting boundaries is a healthy way of containing the wildfire that leads to burnout, and it can be a positive way to use your anger. (I sometimes need that anger to push me to speak up for myself, especially when it feels like the boundary I'm setting might seem "weird" to other people.)

EXERCISE
Emotional Spelunking

One of the fastest ways to get to the root of the emotions you're feeling is to speed-write. Responding to a writing prompt ten times, as quickly as possible, will uncover some buried boundary crossings. Number a page in your journal from one to ten and complete the sentence "I'm angry that _____" as fast as you can. Some of the items from my list might look like this:

1. I'm angry that Mary didn't call me yesterday when she said she would.

2. I'm angry that people at work schedule meetings right over my work blocks. I need those!

3. I'm angry that my boss sent me messages at 9:00 p.m.

4. I'm angry that the wind is so loud and distracting.

5. I'm angry that my cat won't stop attacking my feet when I move them around.

Now that you have a list, repeat the "Things I Can Change" exercise, identifying which items you can do something about and which you can't. I can't do a doggone thing about the wind, but I can shore up my sensory comfort in other ways to offset the discomfort it causes me. I can text Mary and express my disappointment that she didn't call. Or I can use that spurt of anger-fuel to decline the meetings scheduled over my work blocks. (Ooh, it's so satisfying!)

With neurodivergent burnout, using the metaphor of wildfire is a little misleading, because a wildfire becomes a conflagration very quickly, and everything burns all at once. Neurodivergent burnout is more of a slow, smoldering burn under the surface. They are more like "sleeper" fires; they can absolutely ignite and become a full-on wildfire, but because they can lie in wait for a long time, they often take us by surprise. Likewise, neurodivergent burnout can be totally surprising to the people around us. Meltdowns and shutdowns are early warning signs; they are the smoke that we smell even before we can see the flames. Because neurodivergent burnout causes significant and often permanent damage to the person suffering it, it's important to prevent it as much as possible.

However, it's unlikely that you've come to this book at the earliest stages of potential burnout. It's far likelier that you're at least a year or two into the symptoms of burnout and are struggling to see the possibility of life on the other side. When the anger has subsided, and the fires have been contained, there's a new emotion to deal with: sadness.

Floods and Mudslides of Neurodivergent Burnout

When the sky is choked with smoke, and we're receiving text alerts that we need to be prepared to evacuate at a moment's notice, rain is a relief. When the monsoons finally come and dowse the flames, we take a deep breath and allow a glimmer of hope to come in. In this stage of burnout, people say things like "I'm starting to feel like myself again." We feel the despair receding and can see the possibility of a future beyond burnout. However, this is the riskiest stage of the burnout-recovery process. The temptation is to just ramp back up to the life we had before without making any changes. We might expect ourselves to work as many hours or do as many things as we did before our burnout. The danger here is that we'll just keep reigniting the fire the minute we feel better. It is important to take the time to work through this stage, before trying to tackle things "the old way." By spending some time with this stage, you can prevent yourself from reentering the burnout cycle.

As I explained in chapters 1 and 2, the rain that follows wildfires can be massively destructive, bringing mudslides and flash floods. The Flood stage of burnout is about sadness and grief; it evokes the melancholy image of a rainy, gray day or being awash with tears.

If anger provides fuel to create change, sadness tends to drain us of energy. Anger is a more socially acceptable emotion to express than sadness, and it feels *powerful*. Even amid the powerless and hopeless feelings of burnout, anger has a spark to it. Sadness does not; it makes us feel weak.

In many cases, this stage looks like a form of clinical depression. It may very well be that, too. If that's the case, be sure to seek medical attention. (See page 56 for more on how to tell the difference between burnout and depression.) However, it may not truly be depression, but *grief*. While depression's causes are often negative self-talk or internal brain chemistry, grief's cause is a very real loss. Grief is, at its heart, a reasonable emotional response to circumstances of loss. At this stage, having a validating support system with at least one person who can hold space for this loss and validate your feelings is vitally important.

After a wildfire, there are often sections of the forest that are not totally destroyed: trees that are big enough to resist burning, or areas where the wind kept the fire low, perhaps. In a season or two, those sections of the fire scar will bounce back, canopy and all. There are other sections, though, where the fire burned the hottest, unabated by firefighting efforts. In those areas, there will be charred spikes of dead tree trunks dotting the mountainside for years to come. The soil, too, was completely charred in those places, so it will take time for even the smallest seeds to sprout.

This more permanent kind of damage is unfortunately more common to see in neurodivergent burnout than in professional burnout. This is not due to a personal failure or a lack of resilience. This is because neurodivergent burnout causes serious problems. A person's ability to cope with certain sensory stimuli may decline or go away completely.

A person's energy for masking (see page 84) may be depleted. Support needs may increase. Cognitive abilities may be lost entirely. Neurodivergent burnout is devastating. Yes, just as in the forest, some things will come back more quickly than others. But, like the fire scar, it usually takes two or three years to discover what those things may be.

Because of the immediate danger of the post-fire floods and mudslides, now is not the time to assess what has survived and what is literally "scorched earth." At this stage, the first thing to do is to accept and feel the emotions of sadness surrounding the loss of burnout, allowing the rains to fall on our burned inner landscape.

EXERCISE
Feeling Sadness

Number a page in your journal from one to ten and, as quickly as you can, complete this sentence: "I am sad that _____."

While anger calls us to *do* something, sadness calls us to acknowledge *lack*. Something is missing for us. In the case of burnout, that lack is often experienced as a *loss*—a loss of the "old you." That person is gone. In the Regrowth stage, you will explore the new person who is here now, with curiosity and wonder. But before regrowth can begin, you have to fully let go of the person you used to be. That landscape has permanently changed.

EXERCISE
Grieving the Old You

As mentioned earlier, grief is often described as "love with nowhere to go." Sketch or write about the old you—the person who existed before burnout. Highlight the things you loved about yourself. Describe that past person in loving terms. What did they dream of? What were their goals or ambitions? What inspired them? What brought them joy?

Is there anything you can do or bring into your present life to honor that person?

Are there any pieces of that person that you can identify as being gone forever? Can you make a list of things that this person did that you will not be able to do so easily anymore?

RITUAL
Letting Go

Holding your past self in your heart with love is hard. But you don't have to do it alone. Select someone on your support team to do this activity with you.

With a loved one or therapist, tell stories of this previous version of yourself, and talk about things that you used to do or enjoy. Hold hands, cry, and mourn this person. Often, when we are grieving lost loved ones, telling stories together is the best way to honor them.

Sometimes, as a way of grieving, we will place something that they loved in a position of prominence in our home. See if you can find a symbol or talisman of that past self to put somewhere special and visible.

Give yourself time and space to feel sad. Again, this process is not linear. It's very likely that sadness will bubble up again and again as you go through the Regrowth stages—just as it continues to rain long after things begin growing back in the fire scar.

You might notice at this stage that your executive functioning is extremely poor. You might want to get started on a task or a project, but you absolutely cannot make yourself begin. No matter how much energy you expend trying to trick or force yourself to do it, you're stuck. This gets internalized and shamed as "laziness" or "procrastination," but the internal turmoil caused by executive dysfunction is anything but laziness. There are a lot of reasons for executive dysfunction to arise, but repressed emotions are one big culprit. These unexpressed emotions are often completely unrelated to the task at hand, but because they use up so many internal resources, they make it very hard to do anything else. While there are many strategies we can use to sidestep executive dysfunction issues (like gamification, parallel tasking, and setting timers), the underlying cause won't be resolved without some emotional processing. The more you can name and acknowledge your feelings at this stage, the better.

EXERCISE
Overcoming Inertia

The next time you feel stuck or frustrated by executive-function inertia, number your journal from one to ten and complete the sentence "I feel _____" as quickly as possible. Use the list of primary emotions on page 81 if you need to. Now read through your list of sentences and see if you can feel any changes in your body as you read each one. Select the two answers that cause the biggest physical sensation or response. Write at least one page about each of them. Name the emotions, acknowledge your feelings, and think about where they come from. Feel them in your body and breathe deeply a few times.

Following wildfire season in New Mexico, you need to have a plan before the rain begins to prepare for the floods. You should know how the water flows around your house, which roads are usually safe in flash floods, and where you can get to safety if there's a mudslide. Often, public projects ensure that water drainage and diversions are ready to handle the floods. This sort of planning can be undertaken on a meta-phorical level as well. To prepare yourself for the emotional undertow of deep sadness and grief that follows burnout, certain channels need to be excavated well in advance. One such preparation is the establishment of structure and routine.

Because neurodivergent people don't have the neurotypical ability to filter out sensory input or social interactions, even everyday tasks can require a lot of conscious thinking. Establishing structure and routine is a vital way to make those tasks easier when burnout disrupts daily life. This is something that should be worked on together with the people who share your living space. It's usually more effective to fit daily routines around existing structure. Just as it makes the most sense to dig ditches beside existing roads, it's easier to create muscle memory around routines if they are attached to things that are already in place.

EXERCISE
Identifying Daily Problems

Outline the existing structure of your day. Do you have certain routines already in place, such as making coffee in the morning, walking the dog in the afternoon, or going to work or school during certain hours? Those routines become the skeleton you can build more habits upon.

Make a list of the regular, daily problems that you need to solve and things that frequently cause you extra stress. Does clutter cause overstimulation? Do you seem to always miss meals?

Don't try to think of solutions to the problems outlined in the last step just yet. First, assess what can or can't be changed easily (if you need to, revisit the "Things I Can Change" exercise earlier in this chapter). Second, prioritize the ones that can be changed. Which of those items is the most important? Which would have the most impact for reducing your stress levels overall?

Two of the best tools that we have for circumventing executive-dysfunction issues and adjusting our routines are timers and task chaining. Let's first look at timers. We all have heard the advice to set timers for specific intervals to help us focus on tasks. My phone is full of timers at fifteen-minute intervals, and I add a description to each one so I know what the heck the timer means when it goes off. Timers of this sort can help tasks feel more like a game and keep us from getting overwhelmed.

EXERCISE
"Arbitrary" Timers

Recruit everyone who lives in your home for this activity. Set a timer for ten minutes, and make sure the alarm is loud enough to be heard throughout the house. Before you start the timer, say, "Ready, set, go!" Then, for ten minutes, everyone speed-cleans as much of the house as possible. Each person can focus on the parts of the home that stress them out the most—whatever they notice first. Importantly, no one is in charge, there is no list of items to be done, and nothing has to be done completely. This is a race; it's a game. At the end of the timer, everyone stops. You might want to spend two to three more minutes finishing whatever task you were doing, but the key here is to stop and assess together the improvement that was made to the home. Appreciate one another's hard work!

You may find that a weekly ten-minute "speed clean" session is enough to reduce overstimulation and stress. This sort of "gamification" and having a finite timeframe can make the often-overwhelming task of housekeeping a little more manageable.

Arbitrary timers are great for simple, finite tasks. But they work less well for daily routine. This is because once we are used to them, they become easier and easier to ignore. We know that they are arbitrary, and it doesn't matter if we just blow right past them while we do other things. This is where *non-arbitrary* timers can be useful. A non-arbitrary timer is a finite, specific time frame that is limited by an external factor. Machines you regularly use around the house can be useful non-arbitrary timers: the three minutes while the microwave is running, for example, or the fifty-five minutes of a washing machine cycle. We have a task to perform—or a reward—when the timer goes off: our food is ready; we have clean clothes to unload. This gives the timer *meaning*. Further, these kinds of tasks are often already built into existing routines, making it easier to stack other activities on top of them.

EXERCISE
Non-Arbitrary Timers

Make a list of non-arbitrary timed events that happen in your household or in a typical day. Consider the "Identifying Daily Problems" lists you outlined above to help brainstorm these events. Some examples might be:

- Microwaving food
- Running the washing machine or dryer
- Running the dishwasher
- Brewing your morning coffee
- Commuting to work or school
- Waiting in a line
- Waiting for a bus to arrive

The next step is *task chaining*. The idea of task chaining is to build habits around essential daily tasks. For most people with executive-dysfunction issues, task chaining can help circumvent inertia and overwhelm. When task chains become part of daily routines and structures, they often no longer require concentration or conscious thought. You can find yourself doing the task chain without realizing you were performing an entire series of tasks. Building positive, useful task chains can help support you in your daily routine.

EXERCISE
Task Chaining

Make a list of things that you need to do every day (whether you already do them every day or not). Now go back to the list of problems you identified in the exercise "Identifying Daily Problems" above. Are there any daily tasks that might help solve those higher-priority items? For example, if the kitchen mess is overwhelming, managing dirty dishes daily might help solve that. Your list of daily tasks might look like:

- Brushing teeth
- Putting on deodorant
- Feeding pets
- Checking emails
- Going to work
- Washing dishes
- Preparing meals

Put a check mark beside the things that you already successfully do daily. Circle the items that you do not currently do or do not always do. Are there any tasks that obviously go together? For example, brushing teeth and putting on deodorant could be done one after the other: this is a task chain.

Now, look at the tasks that are circled, and think about which ones might resolve some of your highest-priority problems. Can you apply task chaining to incorporate it into your existing routine? Can you use a non-arbitrary timed event to remind you to do it and help shape that routine?

Choose the most important of these circled items, and endeavor to do this one thing for three weeks. If it reduces your stress and resolves emotional issues, then it works for you. Once you feel like the task chain has worked, add in the next one, and then the next, slowly over time.

As an example of all these things in action, I'll explain my own morning routine. I live alone, so I must support myself through any potential stressors, and I had several problems that I needed to solve:

1. Dishes and kitchen mess overwhelmed me, making it difficult to cook a healthy dinner for myself in the evening.

2. I lack strong interoception, so it's easy for me to forget to eat until I'm having problems.

3. Executive dysfunction can make it hard for me to get dressed in the morning.

When I thought about my existing daily routine, I noticed certain things that I'd already built into my morning routine years and years ago. These could provide some structure to help me with challenges I was trying to solve:

1. I make a French press of coffee each morning.

2. I feed the pets and check their water each morning.

3. I let the dog out to pee each morning.

4. I write in my journal each morning while I have my coffee.

My pets are timers and reminders in and of themselves. The dog's urgency to go outside and the cats' demands to be fed are useful to make sure I'm out of bed. By adjusting the existing "let the dog out" task to "take the dog on a walk," I was able to ensure that I'd get dressed in the morning. (Taking the dog on a walk also helps me work outdoor exercise into my day, which helps with self-regulation.)

My coffee-making process is also a non-arbitrary timer. It takes me about twelve to fifteen minutes to boil water, steep the coffee, and so on. I now hide my coffee supplies behind where I've stacked the dirty dishes, which requires me to do them and helps chain the task of washing dishes to my existing "make coffee" task. This non-arbitrary timer gives me the reward of my coffee at the other end, and I clean up the kitchen in that short span of time each morning. Do I get *all* the dishes done in that time every day? Nope. But I get *enough* done to reduce my stress levels and allow myself to cook something later in the day.

I also added another task to my morning routine: making myself a protein shake. I do this while I'm still moving around the kitchen, before I sit down to plan my day. This helps make sure that I'll eat something even when I don't feel like it, making it less likely that I'll have hunger-related problems later. By the time I sit down with my journal and coffee, I've reduced my three biggest stressors.

My morning routine is a structure that supports me even when I'm overwhelmed, stressed out, or otherwise struggling with the rest of my life. It ensures that at the very least, I've gotten dressed, I've gotten some nutrition, I've made the kitchen a mental safe space, and I've cared for all the pets. This is an example of planning ahead for the emotional runoff and turmoil that is part of the burnout-recovery process. The more you can use skills like these to reduce your bigger stressors, the more quickly you can move into the Regrowth stage and find true recovery from burnout.

Regrowth and Recovery After Neurodivergent Burnout

One of the biggest misconceptions people have about burnout is that it's possible to "bounce back" quickly. This is not only highly unlikely but, in the case of neurodivergent burnout, next to impossible.

Neurodivergent burnout is a profound and permanent state of destruction that reaches far beyond workplace burnout and career dissatisfaction. One of the primary symptoms of neurodivergent burnout is the inability to go back to old coping mechanisms. In many cases, it feels as if the way the brain functions has permanently changed. Sensitivities may be heightened, and stress responses, meltdowns, and shutdowns may occur more frequently. It may no longer be possible to participate in social events in the way that you used to.

The Regrowth stage of neurodivergent burnout is about learning how to navigate an entirely new landscape. Some of the big old-growth trees that used to support you are gone forever. You've grieved them, but now how do you move forward? As we explored in chapter 2, the way a forest grows back is through diversity of life. Some plants are encouraged or stimulated to sprout after fire. Some plants have their seeds spread by birds and other animals returning to the area. The newly growing forest is full of lots of little things. The little things grow roots, which will help prevent mudslides next year.

It is easy to be impatient with the little things that begin to sprout for us at this phase of burnout, wanting them to grow faster. We can be eager to rush forward into a new chapter of life. Be patient with this part, and with yourself. It can take time to discover the new normal.

EXERCISE
Assessing Your Forest

Return to the "Creating Your Forest" exercise from chapter 2. (Or do it now, if you haven't already!) Imagine that you are walking through this forest, and again assess what's still growing, and what's no longer there. This time, think more concretely about it; make a list of the things in your life that are truly gone because of burnout. You have the tools to further grieve those now. Then list the items that are still alive: special interests that are still supportive, or foods that still taste good.

Finally, make a note of any tiny glimmers of interest and curiosity, the sprouts that are beginning to grow in the light. Where are you going down rabbit holes of wonder or interest? What sorts of media are you gravitating toward?

This is the time to get curious about yourself and your possibilities. Regrowth takes several years to happen, so be patient with yourself. The walks, routines, and emotional-acknowledgment tools earlier in this chapter will help support you during this time, while you wait to see what develops. If the Fire phase of burnout is mostly about anger, and the Flood phase is about grief, the Regrowth phase is one of *hope*.

EXERCISE
Feeling Hope

Number a page in your journal from one to ten and, as quickly as you can, complete this sentence: "I hope that _____."

One of the things that helps neurodivergent people relax is engagement with special interests. Spending time with special interests can help lower blood pressure and reduce cortisol levels; it's a proven stress reducer. Topics and areas of special interest do change over time, though. Sometimes it's worth reassessing those areas of interest to see if there is something else that should be explored. This is especially true in the Regrowth phase of burnout recovery.

As I mentioned in chapter 1, the first crew to enter a wildfire zone after the fire has been put out is the one that assesses the extent of the damage. They measure how deeply into the soil the burn went and assess the health of the trees that are still standing. Taking a similar inventory of yourself is part of the burnout-recovery process.

EXERCISE
Special Interest Inventory

Create an inventory of your special interests, starting with your earliest childhood memories and moving through to the present day. If you struggle to remember your childhood, consider what kinds of toys or ephemera you collected, or what characters you were emulating in old photographs. Do any of your childhood interests speak to you in a new and interesting way? Do you have any new areas of interest that are on the verge of taking on "special interest" status? How can you foster or nurture these interests to help them grow?

Exploring and fostering areas of special interest does more than reduce stress levels—it also provides clues about the path forward out of burnout. By spending some time with these areas of interest in a meaningful and deliberate way, you may discover ways to change career paths or ways to enhance your self-care and support. You might want to consider taking classes, trying out side gigs, or volunteering around your areas of special interest. Volunteering is particularly useful, because of the emotional well-being that grows from helping others.

The self-care menu you created earlier in this chapter should be well-used by this point in the healing process. Now we're going to put a bit of a finer point on it. In occupational therapy, there is a concept called a "sensory diet." The idea is that certain sensory stimulants fall into three different categories: *alerting, soothing,* and *organizing.* The stimming activities or self-care options we select from our menu may fall into one of those categories. A sensory diet—selecting from one specific section or type of sensory experience—can help you move your mind and body into a different state. This is especially useful if you need to concentrate on work or if you need to self-soothe quickly.

Alerting sensory triggers are things that wake you up. They are great for that energy slump in the midafternoon, or right after waking up in the morning. Alerting foods are cold, crunchy, and/or spicy. (Ice cubes and Altoids fall on my list of alerting foods.) Music with varying rhythms or which is unfamiliar to you can be alerting. Bright lighting, cold temperatures, and wet sensations are also alerting. I've walked outside into dewy grass before to create alertness. Dancing can be an alerting activity.

Soothing sensory triggers are the opposite of alerting ones. These are useful when you're stressed out or overwhelmed, and right before bedtime. Soothing foods are warm and/or sweet, and might have smooth, creamy textures. (One of my favorite soothing bedtime snacks is a little Greek yogurt with a dollop of honey.) Soothing music tends to have long, slow notes and a predictable rhythm. It is usually something you've listened to before. Dim lighting, warm temperatures, and soft textures and smooth textures are also all soothing sensory triggers.

Organizing sensory triggers help jump-start executive function. They are a must-have for the self-care menu, because they can help you get things done when it feels impossible. They are useful to keep your mind on a high-priority task or to help you complete a project. Organizing foods are chewy or crunchy—things that take a lot of rhythmic movement to eat. (Chewing gum is a great organizing food.) Organizing music tends to have a very strong, regular rhythm that allows you to "get into the groove"; I use drumming music or techno beats. Daylight and spending time outside are also organizing. Linear, rhythmic exercise like walking or running can be organizing, as is rocking or swinging. Pressure is another organizing sensation: weighted vests or pressure vests are often used for kids to help them organize their thoughts in occupational therapy—I've used one myself, while working from home.

Do you find yourself already using some of these? Now, let's brainstorm other examples of alerting, soothing, and organizing sensations to add to your self-care menu.

EXERCISE
Rewrite Your Self-Care Menu

Now that you've used it a handful of times, revisit and revise the self-care menu that you created for yourself earlier in this chapter. Add any new alerting, soothing, or organizing "menu items" that could help you in the future. This is an ongoing exercise that will help not only with regrowth, but also with future burnout prevention.

At this point, the forests are growing back. This will take time. A succession of plants will appear over the coming months and years: The first wave is ground cover that grows well in disturbed soil and needs a lot of sunlight. Next, new seeds are spread and begin to sprout, and eventually, a new forest will grow. However, the burned husks of the trees that still cover the landscape make the burn scar more susceptible to future wildfires. The next phase is one of ongoing stewardship and prevention.

Burnout Prevention and the Ongoing Health of Your "Forest"

At this stage, you have experienced the devastation that is left behind after burnout. You know that you have been permanently changed by its destruction. You've had time to grieve those changes, and you have the tools to continue grieving them over time. Some of those tools include:

- An assembled support team (you don't have to stop using this team just because you're recovering)
- Journaling and exercises to gauge your feelings
- A self-care menu to help you take care of your needs when things get stressful
- Skills and tools to help build habits and routines

One aspect of neurodivergent burnout we have not yet addressed is that of *masking*. Masking is like playing a fictional role of yourself, using conversational scripts and other tactics to hide your internal state. Neurotypical folks may also generate personas for specific situations: for example, many people have a "corporate voice" they use on the telephone that is different to the one used with family members. But neurodivergent adults, especially those who are late-diagnosed or undiagnosed, tend to have this persona running all of the time, to a very high degree. Neurodivergent burnout can make it difficult or impossible to mask as consistently as we might be used to doing. This may mean a higher frequency of socially awkward situations and conversations; a reduction in eye contact; or visibly stimming in settings where it may be deemed strange or inappropriate. Masking can be a source of stress because it requires effort and energy, but so can being unable to mask when we'd like to.

Unmasking can help neurodivergent people reduce stress, particularly when they are alone or around trusted loved ones. It's likely that we will still need to mask to feel safe in many situations, so completely unmasking is not likely. However, it's worth the practice and effort it takes to unmask, as it leads to greater self-acceptance and vulnerability with people who care about us. Unmasking takes practice and time. It is a habit that formed in very early childhood, and it's connected to early survival and coping mechanisms. It's largely unconscious—like a form of muscle memory.

EXERCISE
Discerning Masks

When beginning to unmask, the first step is self-observation. When do we feel disconnected from the person we are in the world? When do we feel "shallow" or "fake?" Has anyone in our lives ever accused us of being fake? Make a list of situations when you know you tend to mask.

The next step is to observe and note which people we tend to mask around. These might be people who make us feel unsafe, uncomfortable, or judged.

Now, assess which situations and people in your life are safe to be unmasked around. Are there loved ones with whom you mask regularly, but don't really need to? Are any of the members of your support team on this list? Talk to them about your desire to unmask, and what that's going to mean for your relationship with them. For example, when I had this conversation with my partner, I warned him that unmasking might mean I wouldn't be able to answer questions smoothly in conversation—that I might need time to think about my responses, or I might say something unexpected. This made it possible to not have to pre-script and predict our conversations in advance and allowed me to relax more when we talked.

RITUAL
Trading Masks for Hats

For this ritual you're going to need to gather a few materials. You will need at least one mask; a paper plate with eye holes cut out is enough, if you don't have any old Halloween costumes handy. It is even better if you can find two or three masks. You will also need two or three different hats. Again, a cache of Halloween costumes is useful, but these hats can simply be beanies or baseball caps. The more distinct they are from one another in shape, color, and feel, the better.

First, consider a situation where you now commonly mask, but in which it is safe to unmask: for example, a game night with friends. Put on one of your masks and look in the mirror. Imagine the sights, sounds, smells, and feelings of the place and situation: for example, what snacks do you associate eating at that event? Think about the people you interact with there. Now, looking at yourself in the mirror, take off the mask. Continue looking at your face (eye contact is nice, but not necessary) and breathe deeply. Imagine your sense of safety in that situation without the mask. Hold that sense of safety for a few breaths before moving on.

Next, consider a situation in which you need to continue to do some level of masking to cope or thrive: for example, at your workplace. Again, don one of your masks, and looking at yourself in the mirror, imagine the sensations and feelings you associate with the place and the people who will be there. Now, as quickly as possible, swap out the mask for one of the hats you've collected. What does it mean to switch from a mask to a hat? Hats do not hide our true faces, but they do say something about who we are in each situation. They are the roles that we play in our lives. Look at yourself in the hat and breathe deeply, letting this switch play out in your imagination.

You can repeat these processes as many times as you need to. In some cases, you may wear the mask, look at yourself, and decide that the mask needs to stay put. That's valid, as well. Just sit with that thought and breathe, feeling the safety that comes with wearing the mask in that situation.

Another common source of stress for neurodivergent people, particularly those with ADHD, is *rejection-sensitive dysphoria* (RSD). RSD is the inability to tolerate rejection or failure—whether real or perceived—and it can be extremely stressful; the word "dysphoria" indicates strong or overwhelming pain. RSD can make a person feel like everyone around them is always mad at them or doesn't want to be around them, even when neither is true. Just like people-pleasing and perfectionism (discussed in chapter 2), RSD can contribute to stress around masking and make people burn out more quickly than they otherwise would. This is not something most people can correct on their own, and it should be addressed in therapy. It can also be very helpful to talk to your support team and the people closest to you about how they communicate with you.

EXERCISE
STAR for RSD

While RSD requires professional help to overcome, there are some journaling techniques that can be useful. When we are convinced that someone's behavior is a form of rejection (and it likely isn't), we can journal about it using the "STAR" method. This stands for Stop, Think, Act, and Recover.

The first step, *Stop*, is merely picking up the journal, instead of ruminating, and taking three deep breaths. The next step is to *Think* about the circumstances of the event by writing it down. Try describing it three times:

1. First describe the event as you experienced it.

2. Now, describe it again from the perspective of someone watching it happen from a distance—an objective, outside observer who has no part in the situation.

3. Now, describe it again as if you were a close friend or loved one listening to you talk about the event.

With this act of perspective-taking, you may be able to then decide on how to *Act*, the next step of the STAR method. If your close friend were asking you for help with this situation, what advice would you give them? What would you recommend they do? (This helps you to see, for example, whether an apology is necessary or if you need to better communicate your feelings.)

Finally, after you act on the situation, return to your journal to *Recover*. Describe how you are feeling after the fact: What emotions have come up? How do they feel in your body?

A final important piece of burnout prevention for neurodivergent people is learning to anticipate and prepare for stressful situations that might cause a meltdown. Your self-care menu is an example of preparing in advance for a point in the future where your judgment and ability to make self-care decisions might be impaired. Another example might be a toolkit of sensory-stimulation items. I know that staying in a strange hotel can make it hard for me to relax, so when I travel, I carry a small baggie of sensory self-care items. It includes a tiny LED tea light so I can turn down the lights; a few soothing tea bags for warmth and sweetness; a soft makeup brush for sensory stimming with a soothing texture; and a small essential-oil roller with lavender in it for olfactory stimming with a soothing scent. Because I know airports can stress me out, I pack various forms of ear protection, sunglasses, and eye masks for the plane, and I wear clothing with soft textures. These are things that we may have already learned to do unconsciously, but it's wise to bring that preparatory activity into the conscious mind and make these steps of self-care deliberate.

Another form of preventive preparation is communication with your support-team members. If you know an event is going to cause problems for you, it's easier to set expectations and boundaries in advance, when everyone is relaxed and tensions are not running high. For example, if you know that a concert is going to be hard for you, and it will require recovery time afterwards, it's wise to tell your household members and travel companions that you're going to need a few hours to recuperate the next morning or might need to take a walk after the concert to decompress. Asserting your needs in a realistic way, *before* the event happens, can reduce conflict with people around you and ensure that you get the support you need when you need it.

Just like knowing the early warning signs of a meltdown can help you prevent future meltdowns, understanding the circumstances that lead to burnout can help you prevent future burnout. In my area of New Mexico, we know the weather conditions that make wildfires possible.

Local weather reports, as well as roadside "fire danger" signs, alert everyone to those conditions. If fire danger is high—temperatures are warm, winds are fast and gusty, and the forest and grass are dry—then we know to be extra careful to prevent any stray sparks from starting a blaze. In such conditions, campers may avoid lighting campfires, and controlled burns may be delayed. Likewise, if there are circumstances in your own environment that you know are setting the stage for meltdowns or burnout, it's a good idea to preemptively do some self-care.

While fires can't be prevented entirely (sometimes lightning strikes), we can be alert to the signs that they have started, and we can move to make ourselves safe. By paying attention to emotional cues that something is wrong, we can take proactive measures to isolate the fire and prevent the long-term damage of burnout.

CHAPTER 4

When It's Not
Just Burnout

AS I HAVE MENTIONED several times in previous chapters, burnout at work does not exist in a vacuum. None of us live lives that are free from day-to-day stress and the upkeep of our homes, bodies, and families. Even in the most stable and idyllic situations imaginable, there are still stressors outside of the workplace. Additionally, sources of stress are not limited to the home and office, to our personal spheres of influence and control. Sometimes there are major stressors created by the social, political, and environmental circumstances in which we live, and these also contribute to burnout.

Systemic racism, sexism, poverty, and homophobia are huge contributors to burnout and to illness caused by stress.[1] They can exacerbate the feelings of overwhelm, despair, and helplessness caused by simple professional burnout. A full discussion of these larger systemic and cultural problems is beyond the scope of this book (please see the Resources section for further reading recommendations), but it's still possible to expand our wildfire metaphor to include them.

During the Hermit's Peak/Calf Canyon fire in 2022, there were additional large fires occurring in Los Alamos and Albuquerque at the same time. Virtually all of New Mexico's firefighting helicopters, planes, and personnel were sent to fight these three fires. When yet *another* fire ignited in a different part of the state, it was extremely difficult to divert the same people and equipment to a new location to prevent further loss of life and homes. Similarly, it can be catastrophic to our mental and physical health to have to deal with *multiple* sources of chronic stress over a long period of time. This is when our boundaries and support systems are most important. When wildfire erupts in multiple places at the same time, it requires everyone to not only take care of their own spaces, but also take care of one another. The importance of your support network, community care, and larger systemic action cannot be underscored enough when you are dealing with sociopolitical stressors on top of workplace stress.

Additionally, it's important to remember that actual wildfires can be a source of ongoing stress, as well! The threat of wildfires, or any extreme weather events where you live—as well as general awareness of how the climate crisis is making them worse—can contribute to burnout. It's important to get support and treat yourself gently if these issues are a source of stress for you. In addition to self-care, community care is important when it comes to climate anxiety, just as collective action is needed for climate change. For more help, please see "Climate Anxiety Resources" on page 173.

Disaster Distress Helpline: Call or text 1-800-985-5990

988 Suicide and Crisis Lifeline: Call or text 988

Our wildfire metaphor might also need expanding when it comes to personal trauma; in these cases, it's more like your house itself has burned down, rather than the surrounding forest. Psychologist Donald Kalsched defines trauma as any set of emotions or events that you cannot metabolize.[2] When we are able to metabolize or "process" our emotions, we can identify them, validate them, and then act on them or allow them to dissipate. Trauma occurs when the emotions are too big or the event too large for normal emotional processing to occur. Rather than getting metabolized, the emotions get stuck; we're unable to integrate them into our psyches. This is why some people can experience an event as traumatic, while others do not— even if they're standing right next to them or are members of the same family. Everyone's individual psyche has to metabolize events on its own.

A house fire that happens too close to a forest, given the right conditions, can absolutely spark a wildfire. Similarly, unprocessed trauma can add to the mental and emotional load that contributes to burnout. The self-care and emotional-awareness exercises outlined earlier in this book are intended to help us staunch some of these flames before they burn too out of control. However, as I cautioned in the introduction, they may also stir up traumatic memories and unprocessed events. It is important to use your support network if this happens and not try to push through on your own. If trauma is a part of your personal burnout-fuel mix, it is useful to have a mental-health provider who is trauma-informed.

Navigating Burnout and the Mental Load at Home

Another factor that can contribute to burnout is the work involved in caring for children, loved ones, and the home. It is easy for families to fall into patterns that make certain members of the household bear the brunt of the work required to keep the house moving smoothly. This can lead to feelings of self-neglect, overwork, chronic stress, despair, and helplessness, especially if you are a working full time in addition to being the de facto person in charge of the household. In this situation, the wildfire can spread to threaten your entire household. In my own experience of burnout, I was overworked both at my job *and* at home, and it took a toll on both places; both my boss and my then-husband were impacted by my burnout and chronic illness. I do not think it is a coincidence that my marriage ended in a divorce after the Regrowth stage of my own burnout-recovery process. My hope is that you will be able to use the exercises in this book to prevent that kind of devastation from occurring.

This is part of the reason why it is so important for the members of your household to be on your support team. Acknowledging and recognizing the work and mental load required to run a household is very important. In the corporate world, project managers are paid good money to manage calendars, create schedules, manage priorities, and delegate tasks. It's easy to forget that those jobs are also necessary at home—and they're often stressful. It may be worthwhile to revisit the exercises and rituals in chapter 2 with this perspective. It's very likely that there are unprocessed emotions, unacknowledged boundary violations, and impossible workloads that should be addressed at home as well as at work. The same personality attributes that make us susceptible to burnout at work (perfectionism, people-pleasing, poor boundaries) also make us susceptible to burning out at home.

Financial burdens are also a source of stress and burnout when it comes to our home life. Often the reason we can't leave a toxic employer or quit a job we hate is simply that we can't afford to quit. Housing costs, childcare costs, and other necessary expenses are a source of escalating stress for many of us. If money is a source of stress for you, look into whether financial counseling is available through your employer or local community programs. Many banks and credit unions offer this kind of service for free or can direct you to other resources. Kara Stevens's book *Heal Your Relationship with Money* is another excellent resource; Stevens explains that money decisions are rooted in emotions rather than logic, and explores how underlying childhood lessons feed into the decisions we make with our money.

Consider talking with your support team about your relationship with money, and speak with members of your household about their own. Healing the relationship we have with money can help relieve stress, make it easier to save, and make our money decisions feel more intentional and within our control.

One of my favorite environmental metaphors for a burnout-resilient home life is the beaver dam. Beaver dams create small ponds, but they also spread water out into the surrounding area, creating a small oasis of moisture in their vicinity. When wildfires happen in areas with beaver dams, the fire cannot take hold on the plants and saturated soil, thereby protecting the beaver's home and the area around it. It creates a small, natural containment line. Ideally, our home life should be meaningful, supportive, and restful enough to do the same thing for our burnout. If we are burned out at work, we need not be burned out at home. We can leave the inferno at the office.

EXERCISE
Building Your Beaver Dam

In your journal, write down ten things you can do at home to create an oasis that is separate from your burnout at work. Some examples:

1. When I am asked to volunteer at a school event, I can ask my kids if it's important to them that I be there. Unless they say "yes," I can say "no" to that volunteer request.

2. As fun as my kids' birthday parties are, I do not need them to be overly complicated or have an Instagram-worthy "aesthetic." (The kids really never care as long as they have fun.)

3. I can create a "me-time" hour each day. During that time, the whole family knows that I'm engaged in self-care and not to interrupt me.

Communicate with your support team and your family about your feelings of burnout both at work and at home. It's vital that everyone is on board to help you with your burnout recovery.

When Should I Quit My Job to Recover from Burnout?

Many of the recovery activities in this book are intended to help readers stay in their current work environments. As mentioned above, most people cannot afford to quit a job that is burning them out, so they have to address the issues from within their existing role and workplace. It's not always possible, however, to truly recover from burnout if the workplace itself is constantly reigniting fires.

I have quit a handful of jobs over the years when the workplace was toxic and the conditions leading to burnout showed no signs of letting up. The exercises in this section are intended to help you discern whether you should start sending out résumés or try to stick it out in your current role. The exercise below is intended to be completed after you have already acted on all of the exercises, rituals, and recommendations in chapter 2.

EXERCISE
Workplace Health Check

The following questions are intended to assess how healthy a workplace is and how possible it is to recover from burnout within it. As quickly and honestly as you can, answer the following questions in your journal.

1. Have my boundaries been honored when I have set them with my manager or team?

2. Have there been negative repercussions for my setting limits on my availability?

3. Is there a specific date or deadline after which my workload will decrease?

4. Do I feel like my priorities are aligned with upper management's goals and vision?

5. Is there transparency from upper management?

6. Does management make empty promises that never come to fruition? Are excuses normal?

7. Do I feel supported and appreciated by upper management?

8. Does it feel like information, opportunities, and resources are being hoarded?

9. Is there an environment of favoritism? Double standards? Blaming?

10. Are mistakes seen as temporary setbacks and opportunities to learn, or are they seen as permanent characteristics of a person or their work?

11. Are complaints trivialized or ignored?

12. Do team members and peers collaborate or compete?

13. Are employees' suggestions for improvement or expressions of concern met with retaliation?

14. Is negative feedback only shared in private, one-on-one meetings, rather than in open meetings or on Slack?

15. Is management working to resolve the root issues of my workload problems? (For example, the hiring process for more help is underway.)

16. Does my workplace allow me to make space for spending time with my hobbies or loved ones?

17. Are there negative repercussions for saying "no" at my workplace?

18. Do the mission, vision, and values of this company clearly connect to my own?

Review your answers to the above questions to determine the impact that staying at the same workplace will have on your health and well-being. Generally speaking, workplace culture is dependent upon the examples set by and leadership of the senior leaders and upper management. If they do not support setting boundaries, saying "no," or setting limits, it is unlikely that you will be able to find long-term relief from burnout within that workplace culture. If your direct manager has been unsupportive or unresponsive to your requests for assistance with managing your burnout, this, too, is a red flag. However, a transfer between departments may help with that, rather than leaving the company entirely.

In my burnout journey, the reason I quit one of my jobs was the fact that there would never be an end to the stress. In that position, I was asked to generate shareholder value while also pleasing paying customers and doing what was best for the end user—whose attention and eyeballs on ads were what we monetized. I realized that there was nothing in the company's mission, nothing in its values, and even nothing said in direct conversations with senior leadership that helped determine whose interests should be put first. Instead, it was a constant turf battle between shareholders, customers, and end users. This was, in the end, the reason why I left: The fire could never be fully contained. I'd never escape the cycle. Being honest with yourself about the company, its patterns of behavior, and its expectations of you is vital at this point.

One of the terms you'll hear a lot on social media about toxic workplaces is "gaslighting," and it gets used without context so often that it's begun to lose its meaning. This term refers to the 1944 film *Gaslight,* starring Ingrid Bergman. In the film, flickering gaslights are part of a plot to convince Bergman's character that she's insane and that she can't trust her own senses. An example of gaslighting in a workplace might be when something unpleasant happens and management responds by saying, "That didn't happen." Repeated often enough, the denial of a person's lived experience can make them doubt their own perceptions of their circumstances. It is often subtle and insidious. If you find yourself recording and documenting meetings, events, and verbal agreements more than ever before, it may be a sign that there's gaslighting or manipulation going on.

RITUAL
Gaining Clarity

First, take your deep breaths, and light a candle if you like, setting your intention for the exercise. You may want to gain clarity in your life across the board, or you may want to gain clarity about a specific situation. Just be sure you know what your intention is before you begin. Now grab whatever you use to clean your windows. (You can do this ritual in your house or your car.) Then clean some windows, inside and out. Make sure they are streak-free. The more clarity you need, the more windows you should wash. When you're done cleaning the glass, sit back and take a moment to look at the view out of each window. Notice something beautiful in each view (even if it's small or silly). Then, close the ritual, blowing your candle out if you've chosen to light one. You'll be surprised at the clarity and insights that will bubble up from your unconscious in the next two to three days!

If you are staying in the same role, and at the same workplace, you need to assess whether it still meets your basic needs. To avoid going back into the burnout cycle, your workplace will need to provide you with meaning, satisfaction, and motivation. The following list of basic workplace needs is applicable across a broad range of careers:

1. Safety

2. Security

3. Belonging

4. Purpose

5. Autonomy and Trust

6. Achievement

7. Respect and Recognition

8. Culture of Resiliency and Growth

Safety: Physical safety and well-being are a critical need for any workplace. This may include being provided with safety equipment to protect you from hazardous materials or infectious disease. While some personnel are required to supply their own safety equipment (like steel-toed boots), your employer should ensure that your safety needs are met. If they do not, this could be illegal; at the very least, it should be a reason to consider leaving.

Security: Security refers to the less-physical and less-tangible forms of safety within a job. This includes emotional and psychological safety among coworkers (that is, there is no harassment or bullying). It may also mean having a feeling of security in your job and income. The fear of being fired or laid off at any moment can make any burnout experiences far worse.

Belonging: It is a human need to feel like we belong among our peers. While we need not be liked by all our coworkers, a sense of belonging as part of the team is critical.

Purpose: It is critical to understand why your job matters—to the company, to the department, and to your team. You need this both for a sense of job security and for the work to be meaningful each day. The purpose of your work in the larger world should be a clearly articulated part of the company's mission and vision, and you should understand the role you play within that.

Autonomy and Trust: After our initial onboarding at a new workplace, we need to be able to do our work with autonomy and feel trusted by our peers and managers. This is one of the needs that gets eroded by micromanagement, and it is often an underlying cause of burnout. We all need to feel like we can do our jobs independently without constant monitoring, supervision, or assistance.

Achievement: In addition to achieving regular goals (which are often tied to performance reviews and salary increases) we need to feel like we have done a good job. Doing things we're good at is one of the keys to resilience and thriving. Feeling as if we're unable to accomplish those things—whether because of unclear goals, moving goalposts, or simply not being set up for success—can lead to dissatisfaction and burnout.

Respect and Recognition: We need to feel like we are respected by our peers and managers at work. It's also important to have our hard work recognized; this can take any number of forms, but without recognition, we can feel as if what we're doing is meaningless and doesn't matter to the company.

A Culture of Resiliency and Growth: While this need is a little harder to pin down, it's critical for preventing burnout long term. Markets shift; economies have downturns; business models fail. These are the risks of doing business, and they appear to be happening more frequently than ever before. A workplace that feels secure, operates from trust and respect, and sets up their workers for success should also have a leadership culture that allows for flexibility and change in the face of adversity. When mistakes are made, what is done to learn from them? Is there a culture of blame or a culture of growth?

Use the list above to assess how well your current workplace is meeting your needs. If it feels like most of them are generally being met, then I recommend seeking out a different role within the same company. You can parlay your existing social connections, institutional knowledge, and prior successes into a different role that will be more interesting, meaningful, and exciting. A lateral move between departments can often mean retaining your salary, seniority, paid time off, and benefits. You can use the "Trying on Hats" exercise in chapter 2 to identify other areas of the company that might interest you. Asking colleagues in other departments for quick informational interviews can also be very helpful.

If your workplace does *not* meet the above criteria, then a change in employer will likely be a better long-term plan. In that case, the question is whether you need a new workplace or a different career. As we explored in chapter 2, it's important to first assess which of your biggest strengths have survived your burnout (see "Assessing Your Strengths" on page 67). This next exercise will help you identify the biggest and oldest of the "trees" in your forest, and to see if they are still standing.

EXERCISE
Skills Inventory

Using your résumé, make a list of your skills that draws from the descriptions of your current and past positions. It's best to write these down in the form of verbs that end with "ing"; this will be useful for later exercises. Include any skills that you currently use or that you might consider using in a new role. In your journal, write a few sentences down for your feelings about each of those tasks. It's useful to work quickly on this, to avoid overthinking it. If you aren't sure, check in with how you feel in your body when you consider using that skill. An example might look like this:

Managing a team: I enjoy mentoring and coaching the team. I even like doing performance reviews! I do not like having to lay people off.

Analyzing data: If I never look at another dashboard again in my life, it will be too soon.

Once you've made this inventory, determine which of your existing skills are still alive—skills that you still enjoy doing and that are still meaningful to you. (In the above example, management would be an "alive" skill, while analyzing data probably isn't.) Now, consider things you do in other parts of your life—outside of work—and list the tasks that you enjoy. Some examples:

Video editing for social media: It's fun to figure out how to cut a video down to just sixty seconds. It's a creative puzzle!

Coaching my kid's soccer team: I love watching the little kids learn new skills and grow.

Add these tasks to the list of the skills that are still "alive" at your day job. Now, we're going to look for careers and roles that use as many of those skills as possible. This might mean a complete change in position. For example, if you've previously been a department head, and management and coaching is still viable for you, consider teaching or instructor roles. Refer to the "Ikigai" exercise on page 66 to see if these skills fit somewhere on the diagram. Does a different career idea emerge out of the skills you enjoy using?

If you've realized that your current role is still meaningful, and your current workplace meets your needs, then it's possible that your exhaustion needs to be addressed in another way. Sometimes an extended break or sabbatical may be helpful. Time away may be enough to regrow the landscape.

However, a simple vacation is usually not enough. As a culture, many of us find it difficult to *stop* working.[3] Frequently, we cram our vacations full of things to do and see, even if we're unavailable for work interruptions. When my arthritis flared, I was faced with the possibility of taking short-term disability leave instead of making a complete change in direction. I ultimately decided that this wouldn't help me recover from my burnout, because the root causes were the leadership, workload, and structure of the organization itself; I realized that even with four to six weeks away from work, the stressors would remain. This self-assessment is critical, because if you do take an extended vacation or sabbatical, it's quite common that feeling guilty about having done so will keep you in an unhealthy position even longer after the fact, perpetuating the burnout cycle even further.

On the other hand, if you can take the break fully and really sink into *not-doing*, a vacation or period of leave can be a wonderful way to reconnect with yourself and your deeper feelings and values. For some people, not doing things can feel very frightening. I remember one evening that I was curled up on the sofa in front of a crackling fire. I had a cat in my lap, and the TV remote, my book, and my phone were just out of reach. There was nothing I could do without disturbing the cat; all I could do was sit there. But there was nothing I *needed* to do. There were no fires to put out; even the one in the fireplace needed no tending. Nothing demanded my attention, except an occasional claw from the cat if it woke up and demanded to be stroked. And I remember feeling terrified. Anxiety gripped my chest and made my shoulders clench. I felt guilty for doing nothing. I was braced for the impact of the next demand on my time and attention.

The problem is that if we aren't aware that we are constantly "bracing for impact," and if we aren't ready to deactivate that feeling when we have time to relax, we can *create* the next demand on our time. We can unintentionally generate chaos just because chaos is more familiar than peace. This is a prime moment to practice the "Breathe" ritual from chapter 2, with longer exhales than inhales (see page 47). I have since learned to reassure myself that it is okay to be content in those moments. It is okay to be bored. It is okay to be peaceful. There is no other shoe that is about to drop, and I don't need to create a new to-do list. I can just *be*.

EXERCISE
Human Being (Not Human Doing)

Try not-doing. The first time you do this, do not use any distractions. No television, no music, no social media, no books. Just find a comfortable place to sit and *exist*. For at least thirty minutes, do not even write in a journal. Take three breaths, making your exhale longer than your inhale. Then just observe. Observe the world around you. Observe your thoughts. Observe your emotions, and observe where you feel them in your body. Do you feel stressed? Anxious? Curious? Peaceful? After this half hour, journal about your experience of doing nothing. Write down how it made you feel.

Are there any old or erroneous beliefs that are behind those feelings? Some examples might be:

- I will get in trouble if I just sit here.

- I'm not worthy of love if I'm not helping my family.

- I should be doing something productive.

- This is a waste of time.

Sometimes, these beliefs are tied to old work ethics that haven't served us well or that led to burnout. Sometimes, they're due to negative core beliefs about yourself that you might need to discuss with a therapist. Sometimes, it's just habitual. We are so used to numbing out that we often aren't comfortable spending time with our own thoughts.

I recommend doing this exercise more than once to see if you have resolved any of those feelings or if they bubble back up again and again. The next time you have the opportunity to try not-doing again, select one form of sensory input that you find soothing and pleasant. I sometimes sit outside and watch the wind in the trees or listen to the birds, or I'll watch the fire in the fireplace. Listening to music—and only listening to music—is another great option here, as it gives your senses something to pay attention to while you do nothing. See what emotions arise with that sensory input while you do nothing. If it felt stressful to you the first time you tried this exercise, does it still feel that way?

While it's great to do this exercise on vacation, it's important to practice it on a regular, ongoing basis. How can you work not-doing into your daily or weekly routines? What emotions or beliefs do you need to work through to make that a comfortable idea?

How Do I Prevent Burnout at a New Job?

If you've determined that your current workplace isn't healthy, but the kind of work you do still feels meaningful, you may now be looking for a similar position or role at a new company. As you start your job search, it's important to keep in mind how you can proactively prevent future burnout when you start a new role somewhere.

The first step of conducting a job search is self-assessment. In the previous section, we identified basic human needs we should expect to have met at any workplace: safety, security, belonging, purpose, autonomy and trust, achievement, respect and recognition, and a culture of resiliency and growth. These are the bare minimum requirements you should be looking for. You will also have requirements that are individual to you and your specific needs. These may be around the physical workplace or space: for example, you may need hybrid or remote options, an office with a door, or the ability to wear headphones at work, or you may have parking or commute concerns. You may also have additional needs when it comes to company culture, such as access to a gym in the building, or ensuring that meetings always have agendas and stated desired outcomes. Most people have minimum requirements around paid time off and benefits, or other areas of compensation. The type of company itself may matter to you—do you prefer working for a nonprofit? A start-up? A large company? A small business?

> **EXERCISE**
> **Envisioning the New Job**
>
> Imagine you are going to work on your one-year anniversary at your new position. Take a few deep breaths, and try to hold this image in your mind for a moment or two. Then write at least three full pages in your journal about that day. Where is the job? What is the commute like? What does a normal workday look like? How do you feel sitting at this job? Who are you working with? Include, if you can, descriptions that use all five senses. What does your body feel like as you imagine this?
>
> Now, make a list of the things that you want and need from a new workplace based on the previous inventory you've taken in the exercises above, including your own preferences for space, team, culture, and compensation.

In the "Skills Inventory" exercise earlier in this chapter, you listed the activities you currently do that are meaningful and fulfilling to you. If those activities are things you're doing at work or in a volunteer role, make sure that they are captured in your résumé. You're using that résumé to get the job you want—so be sure to reflect what's the most important to you there. Consider removing things—however relevant to your experience—that you no longer want to focus on or do.

Now, you can begin a job search. Using those activities that are the most meaningful to you as a starting point—you can even use them as search terms—start looking for potential new employers within your network and online. When you start homing in on a few companies, there is homework you can do before you even begin the application process. Tools such as Glassdoor (www.glassdoor.com) are a great way to gauge workplace culture and employee satisfaction. Keep in mind that more reviews will be written by people who are unhappy at their jobs than people who are pleased with their employers. However, a discerning eye will notice when multiple reviews cite similar problems. Look for the common causes of employee dissatisfaction and burnout: Are workloads too high? Is there no trust, respect, or autonomy? Do people feel unsafe?

In addition to review sites, look at the company website, particularly the "about" pages. If it's a public company, look at the members of the board, as well. Is there a truly diverse and representative blend of genders, ages, and backgrounds at the highest levels of the company? This can often hint at how well a company will meet your personal requirements. For example, a company with only men on the board or executive team may not see any value in having progressive maternity leave or family care policies. A company with this sort of leadership may have underlying cultural penalties when parents need to take time off to care for a sick child. While this isn't enough of a red flag to determine whether you should take an interview or not, it's a good data point to keep in mind.

Now, look at news with the company's name attached. Are there any scandals, layoffs, or other newsworthy events that might impact the day-to-day world of working there? Companies that are in financial trouble are more likely to burn out employees, because they will have hiring freezes—and demand more work out of fewer people to make up the difference. If the leadership team appears in negative news stories, it can signal a volatile work environment. If it's a small or local business, reading Yelp or social-media reviews is also useful.

Some companies have longer and more complex interview processes than others. Sometimes, you may have a series of interviews with an HR representative, potential peers, or even executive leadership.

It's wise to prepare some questions for each of these kinds of interviews that will help you discern whether or not it's a toxic workplace. Return to your self-assessment, and the list of things you require, and brainstorm some possible questions you can ask. Remember, job interviews are like dates—you're *both* looking to see if you're compatible.

Some questions can be answered without asking them outright. A visit to the workplace location itself may answer specific questions around commute and parking, for example. If you have concerns about physical safety, you can look for a "number of days since injury" sign. This can also help guide the questions you'll ask in your interview, such as, "How often are employees injured working in this facility? What usually causes injuries?" Keeping your eyes peeled while you're visiting the workplace can help prompt other questions as well: for example, if you see a publicly displayed calendar featuring bikini-clad models, you might want to ask about the company's sexual harassment policies.

One critical thing to watch for in your interview process is any sign of exhaustion and burnout among the people actively interviewing you or the people you see in the workplace. Do people have dark circles under their eyes? Do they sigh heavily when you ask tough questions? Do they allow notifications or phone alerts to interrupt the interview? Do they seem to lack enthusiasm? If you notice these signs in only one person you meet, then it may be just that one person at the company who is burned out. If you spot these signs in several people, *run.*

Also, notice how they treat your physical needs through the interview process. Do they offer you a glass of water? A place to sit down? If you're interviewing with a number of people on the same day, do they give you the opportunity to take a break or decompress, or do they force-march you from place to place? These are also signs for how the company and team might handle your having a physical body with physical needs (such as taking sick days or time off).

It's common to ask questions about compensation, benefits, and paid time off in the interview phases. It's harder to ask questions that address underlying company culture, job security, or other needs we're looking to fulfill. If you've read on Glassdoor or in the news that a company has reported layoffs in the last six months or so, it's a good idea to ask about it. It's perfectly within reason to say, "I saw that two departments were recently laid off. Why are you hiring for this role, now?"

If you have the opportunity to interview with potential cowork-ers, that's a great time to ask specific questions about the person who would be your manager. This might include questions about how the manager approaches work-life balance and off-hours availability, or how they respond to setting boundaries or limits. It's also valuable to ask a question about how that manager handles delegation—that is, are they a micromanager? One of my favorite questions to gauge this is, "Does the manager trust the team?" Even if the answers you get are polished and measured, the question often surprises people enough that you'll catch flickers of the truth in their facial expressions before they respond.

A few more sample questions include:

- What is the policy for ongoing professional development? Is there a budget for further training?
- How are employee achievements recognized or celebrated?
- What is the standard policy for promotions?
- How quickly is the 401K match vested?
- If there is tension between different parties (for example, between customers and shareholders), who is given priority?

Finally, before accepting a job, repeat the "Checking In" exercise in chapter 2, placing your hand on your abdomen, chest, or forehead, and asking your gut, heart, and head to weigh in on the opportunity (see page 65). Your gut and heart can intuitively pick up on red flags and telltale signs of toxicity better than your head can. Even if the money is great and the commute is a dream, let your gut and heart lead the decision to take or pass on a job. Your instinct is going to be better at reading the room in an interview than your logical mind will be. Those flickers of facial expressions may have been inscrutable to your thinking mind, but your instinct caught them and interpreted them flawlessly. Trust that.

If you find a workplace that you think is a good fit, and you're ready to get started in your new role, there are additional things that you can do to prevent burnout. Just as I must ensure the trees and yard are trimmed every fire season to prevent damage from potential wildfire, you can implement some "burnout hygiene" right from the start. My grandma's career advice to me on starting a new role was "don't start doing anything you don't want to keep doing every day." So, with that in mind:

- From day one, get into the habit of turning off email or message notifications at the end of the workday and on weekends. Don't ask your manager if this is okay—just do it. If they push back (and they likely won't), then reinforce the boundary if possible.

- Get into the habit of using your one-on-one meetings with your supervisor to review your tasks and goals, and highlight when your workload exceeds your working hours. Proactively ask for their help with prioritizing activities so that you know what can shift from week to week.

- Find out what the paid holidays and paid-time-off policies are for new hires. Make sure you have at least one long weekend coming up in the next four to six weeks to decompress.

- Give yourself a lot of grace. It takes three months to understand a new role at all, and six months to be able to do it without help. It takes a year to be able to do it well.

Job changes are stressful, even when and if they are good changes. Make sure that you're keeping your self-care and support systems in place for at least six months following the start of a new role.

When Should I Change Careers Completely for Burnout Recovery?

Sometimes there is nothing left of the forest once the wildfires have gone out. The canopy is gone, and only black, lifeless trunks remain. If this is how you feel about your work, a complete change of career may be the only way to exit the burnout cycle. Career changes are not easy, and they often require a sacrifice in terms of income, seniority, and experience. Sometimes—but not always—they require a return to school. They can be daunting to undertake, especially when your income is needed to keep the household afloat. For all of these reasons, it's rare for people to change careers entirely.

The first step in this process was the "Skills Inventory" exercise earlier in this chapter. Clear self-knowledge and self-awareness are critical for this activity. Just as foresters need to know which trees will come back to life in later seasons and which are simply wrecked trunks to be taken down, you will need to assess the damage and discern what still has life and possibility. You might find yourself revisiting many of the exercises in chapter 2, especially the "Ikigai" and "Assessing Your Strengths" exercises (see pages 66 and 67) through this process of letting go of your past career and envisioning a new one.

Do you already know what you want to do next? Many of us have had our ideal career in mind since we were five or six years old. Or maybe you've already "tried on hats" (see pages 68–69) and found that your energy, enthusiasm, and interests are flowing in a particular direction.

EXERCISE
Skills Gap Assessment

First, do an online search for the work you already know you want to do, and research the skills necessary to do the job. Look at entry-level or junior-level job descriptions and make a list of the required skills and experience listed there. These are the skills you'll need to add to your inventory.

Next, review your own résumé. Highlight any skills and experience that are relevant to your new, desired career. Compare this with the job descriptions you've found: are there any skills needed for these positions that you already have, but which may not currently be on your résumé? For example, I may not have included line editing as a specific skill on my résumé if I've primarily been applying to copywriting jobs. However, if I have that skill, and I want to shift to a career as an editor, I might add more details of my line-editing experience. This is the first step in drafting a career-change résumé.

Finally, make a list of the skills and work experience that you don't currently have, but which you'll need to get the job you want. This is the "skills gap," which will inform your next steps.

Once you have completed a clear and honest skills-gap assessment, then you can create an action plan to get the necessary experience to make the move. You can do this any number of ways. Yes, going to school is an option, but you can also volunteer, job shadow, or sign up for gig work. If your current workplace has roles that use the skills you need, see if an interdepartmental transfer or cross-training exercise would be possible. Sometimes, you can teach yourself the skills you need: for example, you can gain computer or digital-marketing skills by setting up your own website or e-commerce shop and learning by trial and error. This also gives you a preliminary portfolio you can use later.

The other thing that will support this kind of move is networking. Joining online groups, newsletters, or in-person meetups can help you meet people who are doing what you want to do. Talking about the possibilities and hurdles in front of you can be very useful, especially as you're growing a new skill set. These folks may be able to help train you, pass gigs your way, or even tell you who is hiring. Networking is a difficult thing to do, but as humans, we really enjoy helping other people. Asking others to help you is giving them an opportunity to feel good about themselves.

Often, the biggest hurdle to making a drastic career change is financial. It's not unusual for people to get laid off during or after burnout. Even if you never verbally express your burnout at your current workplace, managers can sense the disconnection, dissatisfaction, and unhappiness that you're bringing to your work every day. If and when layoffs happen, that lack of enthusiasm can put a burned-out person's name at the top of the list. Many people who get laid off at this juncture consider it a gift. It's an opportunity to revisit, rethink, and reconsider. However, if finances are tight, they may have to toss themselves back into the flames, doing the same role at a different company. This is why it's important to have a financial plan.

EXERCISE
Thinking About Finances

Get real with numbers. Sit down with your spouse, accountant, and/or anyone who has a stake in your household finances. Write out your current monthly expenses, income, and savings. Working together, look at your budget and expenses to answer these questions:

1. What is the amount of money you need to have in savings to cover your household needs for three months? Six months? Do you have that in savings? If not, how much more would you need to save?

2. What is the absolute lowest amount of money you need per month to cover your basic expenses? Consider this a temporary exercise; think of it as a six-month period during which you would be forgoing dining out, cancelling streaming services, and not contributing to savings or retirement accounts.

3. Taking that absolute lowest, "keeping the lights on" number from the previous question, what would your rock-bottom annual salary or hourly wage need to be, accounting for taxes?

4. What debt would you need to pay down or pay off to feel comfortable without income for a few months?

Next, create a savings plan that feels comfortable for everyone. Ideally, this plan will enable you to save enough to cover six to nine months of your "bare minimum" expenses. Now, get everyone on board to get that savings-and-debt-reduction plan in place. Post a timeline where you can all see it and have regular check-ins for the coming months. This will be a foundation for your exit strategy.

If you're burned out, your family and household are suffering collateral damage. Do not think that you are asking "too much" of anyone to change financial goals and spending habits in the short term to affect a career change.

Most career changes require a lateral move or a reduction in income, and they can take a few months to come to fruition. By knowing your bare-minimum salary, you will be better able to assess potential alternative positions. By setting up a savings and debt plan for a temporary leave of absence, you will not only be more comfortable in the event of a layoff, but you will also have the space and time to truly explore your new work and career possibilities.

After I set up my financial plan, it took me eleven months to pay off debts and build savings before I could comfortably leave my full-time job. I then used that savings to give myself time to pursue passion projects and explore where my energy and enthusiasm led me. Once I identified my new career direction, a normal week included making networking calls, talking to mentors, and gaining work experience in the field I wanted to move into. I did temporarily set up a few consulting gigs in my old career of digital marketing, which helped to boost income. But I tried to focus on getting even low-paying or temporary gigs that would move me in the direction of my dreams while also supplementing my budget.

Now, it's also possible that you're burned out and know you need to change careers, but you don't know what it is you want to do instead. Revisiting the exercises in chapter 2 for regrowth and self-discovery is a useful first step. Drawing your forest, planting seeds, and revisiting your ikigai diagram are great places to begin. After you've done this, and perhaps visited a labyrinth, it's time to do some deep inner exploration.

We have the tendency to live "in our heads" when we are working too much and resting too little. We may be a little dissociated—where our body feels unreal, disconnected from our heads, or superfluous to our existence. The next several exercises will help you feel more embodied, relaxed, and grounded.

RITUAL
Get Grounded

When people talk about *grounding*, what they really mean is feeling fully present in the moment and in your physical being. There are many ways to get grounded. I'm offering two tools to try; if they don't work for you, please don't get discouraged. I recommend continuing to try grounding techniques until you find the one that reliably leaves you feeling calm, centered, and present. The first technique is perhaps easier and more effective, but it requires a safe, quiet outdoor space. The second technique can be done anywhere.

Technique 1: Take your shoes off and stand with bare feet in a patch of soft grass or soil. Take three deep breaths, focusing on nice, long exhales. Feel the sensations of the earth below the soles of your feet, the way the air feels traveling in and out of your nostrils, and the sun or wind on your skin. Imagine, while you stand there, that roots are growing out of the bottoms of your feet and into the soil below you. Feel how supported you are by the earth. Imagine the roots you've grown drawing up helpful water and nutrients. After a few more breaths, assess how you feel. Are you a little more relaxed? Calmer? Are you in the present moment, or are you still distracted by other things? I recommend staying there and repeating the exercise until you are fully present with your body and the present moment.

Technique 2: Sit in a relaxed position. This can be cross-legged on the floor or a yoga mat, or it can be in a chair, with your feet flat on the floor. The important part is that the position should make you feel secure and supported, and you should be comfortable holding it for three to five minutes. Close your eyes and focus your attention on your breath. Do not try to change your breath; simply observe how it feels in your body, whether it is deep or shallow. Place your hands on your abdomen just under the belly button, imagining a little bowl or pot resting inside your belly. Breathe deeply, imagining yourself filling this pot with fresh air. The air swirls around inside the pot and then flows like steam out with the exhale. After about three breaths, you will be able to imagine that something is filling the pot with golden light, each inhale depositing a little more light inside the pot. When the pot is full, move your hands to cup or hold the pot in the space before your abdomen. Flex your hands a few times to feel it thrumming and alive in your hands. What do you want to do with your pot full of golden light? Sometimes, it feels good to press it into your chest to fill your heart space. Sometimes it feels better to thrust it away, and out into the world, to relieve excess energy. Sense what your body needs you to do with the ball of golden light and follow your intuition. Now, open your eyes and scan your body, focusing again on your breath. Do you feel calmer? More relaxed? Are you in the present moment and in your body fully?

Now that you're grounded, take up your journal for a spelunking tour of your own unconscious depths. These next exercises take a lot of time. The first time you approach them, feel free to just begin them and get the general idea, and then set aside thirty minutes every day to keep working on them. Each day, repeat your grounding exercise before writing.

EXERCISE
Earliest Selves

In your journal, write each of these headings at the top of its own page:

1. When I grow up, I want to be . . .

2. My favorite toys and games

3. My go-to fantasies and daydreams

4. Feedback and opinions

On each page, brainstorm a "mind-map" of ideas. These may connect to one another later, so leave a little space between your answers, and don't worry about being too linear. These are not lists, but rather constellations and star maps. On the first page, beginning with your earliest memories, write the jobs you wanted to have as a child. Every time an adult asked you what you wanted to be when you grew up, how did you answer? In kindergarten? In third grade? On the second page, write about your favorite toys and games as a child; on the third, write your most common fantasies and daydreams. If you break this exercise into several days, try to sit with a specific age each day, working from your earliest memories to your late teens.

On the "feedback and opinions" page, write down what parents, grandparents, and even peers and siblings said about your dream jobs, your favorite games, or any fantasies you may have shared with others. These opinions may be incorrect, invalid, or even cruel or mean-spirited. For example, when I was ten, a teacher said to me, "You'd be good in sales; you never take 'no' for an answer!"

Don't rush this exercise. You may spend several days filling these pages in and still return to them weeks later with another memory that has surfaced. There is no need to analyze or interpret these memories at this time.

The information from our earliest selves is invaluable, but it's not set in stone. If you wanted to be a rock star when you were five, that does not mean you need to go buy an electric guitar. (But it might be a fun hobby to take up!) These layers of your young life are important subterranean pieces that may help you figure out a new career path.

After doing the previous exercise, take a red pen and go back through the page of feedback and opinions offered to you by adults and peers. Decide which of those elements of feedback you wish to retain and internalize, and which of them you reject. I recommend discussing the rejected elements with a therapist or a trusted member of your support team to see if you've unintentionally taken some of those things too much to heart. Knowing what to discard can be as important as knowing what to keep and cherish.

EXERCISE
Taking Inventory of Joys

In your journal, write each of these headings at the top of its own page:

1. Things I'm very good at doing

2. Things I enjoy doing

3. Places I enjoy visiting/being

Fill these pages in the same way as the previous exercise, this time focusing on who you are right now rather than who you were as a child. How do you enjoy spending your time? What do you wish you were doing? Take your time on this exercise as well. Let your thoughts bubble up over the course of a few days, and jot down your answers as they come to you.

   If you don't think you can list anything in the "things I'm good at doing" category, revisit the "Personal Strengths" exercises in chapter 2. Remember, doing things we're good at is key to satisfaction and resilience; identifying our strengths is critical at this phase.

   By spending a few days with these grounding and mind-mapping exercises, you may begin to see patterns taking shape. It's okay if you don't! It may be enough for you to just have a glimmer of your new career idea.

   If you have a good sense of your new career path, I recommend the "Trying on Hats" exercise in chapter 2 and seeing how it feels to explore that new activity or work. If this process has left you feeling like you're seeing a lot of stars, but you still can't find the constellations, continue with the next exercise.

EXERCISE
Drawing Constellations

Ideally, this exercise should be done on a large sheet of paper or posterboard. In a pinch, taping six pieces of printer paper together will do the trick.

   For this exercise, you are looking specifically for action words that describe doing something. I particularly like to use gerunds—a verb form ending in -ing—for this work.

1. Start by looking at the "things I enjoy doing" list in your journal, and identify some of the main categories you see, looking for words that indicate action. Now write down these words on your big sheet of paper, and circle them; for example, "Performing" might be one of the words that I've circled on my page.

2. Now, go back through all seven of the pages in your journal for the "Taking Inventory of Joys" and "Earliest Selves" exercises. Look for items and concepts that relate to the key categories in your circles. Write these around the circle and draw lines to connect them. So, "Performing" may have a spoke coming off it that connects the word "storytelling," which was also on my "things I enjoy doing" list. On my "when I grow up" list, I also wrote that I wanted to be a rockstar and an actress; I can now translate those into action words, like "singing" and "acting." I'll write those down as subcategories of "Performing" as well. If you want to get super fancy, you can color code your different categories and subcategories.

3. Use your color code or some other method to "check off" elements on the lists that have been incorporated into the bigger picture.

4. Look again at your seven pages of ideas. Are there any items that haven't been accounted for in your larger map of words? (Ignore any items on the "feedback" page that you have rejected.) For example, I also wanted to be an astronaut and a marine biologist as a kid, and my favorite toys and games included a microscope and a chemistry set. To incorporate those into my big mind-map, I added the categories "Exploring" and "Experimenting." The spokes coming off of those circles indicated both my childhood interests and activities I enjoy doing now, like baking, that speak to that scientific curiosity.

Now you have a set of categories and concepts that can inform what your next career might be. This poster can provide a valuable picture of what work may be meaningful, enjoyable, and fulfilling for you. Spend some time with the large "hub" categories that have been created, and daydream or imagine what it would be like to do those things as a career.

You may have noticed that these exercises all require a lot of time; I've recommended taking weeks or months to work on them rather than a few minutes. This is because you are looking for signs of life in the soil, and unconscious messages take time to germinate and sprout. It may require a few nights' sleep and a handful of strange dreams to find the answers to some of these questions or unearth the memories you're looking for.

In this final exercise, we're going to make a list of potential changes for the direction of your career. Look at the mind-map you created in the last exercise, and create a long list of possible job titles or career paths that combine as many of your categories as possible. Look for the constellations of multiple words—categories that connect to each other. For example, while I like experimenting, I can't really both do scientific experiments and perform on stage. Or could I? After all, Bill Nye does it!

Be as creative and optimistic in this next exercise as you can allow yourself to be. You can pull yourself down to reality later.

EXERCISE
When I Grow Up, I Want to Be . . .

List your top ten dream jobs. Take time to imagine what each one would feel like and what a day working in that job might entail.

The next step is narrowing down the list of possibilities. The skills-gap analysis you did earlier is a valuable follow-up to this exercise; try doing it again now to help guide your next steps in creating a large career pivot. Look for the career idea that offers the best blend of leveraging your existing skills, providing financial income as required by your situation, and feeling exciting and interesting to you. If these exercises fall flat and fail to give you a clear idea for your next step, consider speaking with a professional career counselor.

Burnout and Chronic Illness (Including Long COVID)

My personal journey with chronic illness began with psoriatic arthritis, which brought with it debilitating fatigue, brain fog, pain, and skin problems. Though I'd had symptoms since 1998, my illness was not diagnosed or treated until 2017, when a severe flare made it impossible for me to work. Because I enjoy having the illusion of control over my health and body, I searched for triggers that I could avoid, I went on extreme diets, and I read a lot of books. Several of these books helped me realize the connection between my stress, my burnout at work, and my chronic pain, including *The Body Keeps the Score* by Bessel van der Kolk and *When the Body Says No* by Gabor Maté. (Note: I do not recommend reading these books without having an active relationship with a therapist. *The Body Keeps the Score,* in particular, is written for physicians and can be very triggering to readers who are dealing with trauma.)

My illness arrived very early in my burnout journey. It became a major part of my life just a year after I'd begun writing in my journal that work was soul-killing and soul-crushing. Had I listened to my body—truly listened—I could have cut my burnout-recovery process down by several years. Instead, I continued to push beyond my own energy levels and capacity. I traveled once a month between Atlanta and Los Angeles to attend school and work functions. I continued to work at full speed, without boundaries and without self-care or self-acknowledgment. I was in the Fire stage of my burnout, and my chronic illness was like a burning, falling tree that lit more trees on its way down, or a gust of wind that helped the flames jump across containment lines.

In some ways, the physical aspects of my chronic illness were also like sirens wailing in the night or an orange sky clogged with smoke and ash, alerting me to the present, ongoing, and serious danger of burnout that I was facing. Burnout can be easy to ignore; severe joint pain is less easy to ignore. Needing a stool to sit down in the shower because standing for ten minutes was nearly impossible—that is not ignorable.

Since the COVID-19 pandemic began in 2020, the appearance of long COVID as a new form of chronic illness has led many people to more closely evaluate their work and their commitments in light of their drastically reduced energy levels. Some people suffering from long COVID have also reported reduced intellectual abilities due to the brain fog caused by the infection. While the medical community still does not have a firm grasp on long COVID, we know that it is a form of post-viral chronic illness similar to chronic fatigue. The biggest risk factors seem to be repeated COVID-19 infections and a return to activity, work, and exercise before fully recovering. This means that those caught in the burnout cycle—feeling compelled to be more productive and more active, despite being sick—are also more likely to suffer long-term problems from illness.

Long COVID and its long, slow recovery process requires rest. It requires time and patience. Many people I've spoken with who are recovering from long COVID are reevaluating their work, their boundaries, their limits, and their priorities. Many of the exercises and rituals in this book aim to assist in that reevaluation.

In the field of depth psychology, we often consider physical symptoms to be something that the body is expressing on behalf of the unconscious—something that we are unaware of or have been unable to express. Sometimes, these symptoms are the body's way of setting our boundaries for us and letting us know what we need. To make sure that we are getting our needs met, we have to reconnect with our bodies and honor their messages. This next ritual is aimed at helping you reconnect with and provide care to your body.

RITUAL
Dry Brushing

For this ritual, you will need a dry brush: a medium-coarse, short-bristled brush that is intended for exfoliating the skin. (These are sold at relatively low prices in supermarkets, drug stores, and places with bath and beauty products.) Just before getting into the shower, take a few deep breaths and then use the dry brush all over your skin, starting with your feet. This quick sweeping process doesn't take long. Always brush toward the heart: move up from the feet and hands toward the torso, and then down from the neck and shoulders. Do not dry brush the face, inflamed skin or wounds, or any areas that feel too sensitive. I recommend repeating this exercise every time you shower for a few weeks. It is an act of self-care and self-love that stimulates the entire surface of the skin in a gentle way. It has been proven to help with feelings of dissociation or disconnection from the body, when performed over time.

It is my sincere wish that this book prevents others from burning out to the point of chronic or long-term illness. Stress is a trigger for flares of chronic conditions. In my case, stress at work was what finally tipped me over into constant chronic pain. The following self-assessment is designed to help you understand how stress affects your personal risk of long-term illness. Hopefully, it can help you prevent it.

Questionnaire: Assess Your Stress Risk for Illness

For the following items, give yourself 1 point for "no" answers, and 5 points for "yes" answers. If your response is "sometimes" or "maybe," assign 3 points. These areas of stress and risk are divided into four categories: acute stress, chronic stress, physical red flags, and mitigating factors. *Acute stress* means extremely high levels of stress that usually have an end in sight. Acute stress can be caused by change, even if the changes are good—such as getting a new job or getting married. *Chronic stressors* are things that do not go away after a period of adjustment. *Physical red flags* are signs your body is giving you that you must slow down and manage stress better. And finally, *stress-mitigating factors* are things that might help relieve any of those other kinds of stress.

Acute Stress Levels

- I do not feel safe in my own home.
- I do not feel like my job is secure for the next six months.
- I do not feel like my living situation and home are secure for the next six months.
- I do not feel like my finances are secure for the next six months.
- I've lost my job in the last three months.
- I have changed positions at work or changed jobs in the last six months.
- I have moved homes in the last six months.
- I have had a drastic change in my immediate family in the last year (marriage, birth of a child, divorce, death, incarceration, etc.) Give yourself 5 points for each one.
- My home or family was impacted by a natural disaster in the last year.
- I have been injured in the last six months (for example, a broken bone or an injury from a car accident).

Chronic Stress Levels

- I am a member of a minority group: this includes race, ethnicity, gender expression, sexual orientation, neurodivergence, age, and other minority categories. Give yourself 5 points for each one—systemic issues create chronic stress and often mean you lack support.

- When I think about the sources of my stress, it feels like there is no end in sight.

- I have been diagnosed with a disability, chronic pain, or a chronic illness.

- I do not have control or influence over the things that are causing my stress.

- I do not have adequate support from people in my life (including family, coworkers, and managers).

Physical Red Flags

- I have a hard time concentrating or focusing on things I need to do.

- I feel like I'm always coming down with some virus or bug.

- I take antacid, anti-diarrhea, or laxative medicines frequently or daily.

- I do not sleep well at night, or even when I sleep well, I don't feel rested in the morning.

- I get frequent headaches.

- When I take time away from work, I often come down with a cold or bug.

- My doctor is concerned about my blood pressure, cholesterol levels, or blood sugar levels.

- I have gained or lost more than twenty pounds in the last three months.

- My libido has changed dramatically in the last three months.

- I have allergies or a skin rash that will not clear up or go away.

Potential Stress-Mitigating Factors

- I do not have a regular workout or exercise schedule.

- I do not have a regular meditation practice.

- I do not regularly practice my hobbies.

- I do not regularly schedule time away from work.

- I consume more than 200 micrograms of caffeine per day.

- I consume more than three glasses of alcohol per week.

- I consume drugs or tobacco in any form.

- I do not have safe people or places in my life to express my emotions.

- I am a perfectionist.

- I do not feel safe or comfortable sitting still and doing nothing or resting.

Scoring: Add up the total number of points for all sections above.

If your score is 35 to 100: You are managing your stress pretty well, and you are probably not at risk for developing a new chronic illness. Review your areas of stress where you answered "5" above with your support team.

If your score is 100 to 150: You are at an elevated risk for chronic illness caused by stress. Now is a good time to ensure that you are building stress-mitigation factors into your daily life. Be sure to discuss your stress levels with all members of your support team.

If your score is greater than 150: You are at an extremely high risk for heart disease, stroke, or chronic illness. Please review your scores with your doctor and support team, and recruit more support as soon as possible.

Ultimately, our bodies and our psyches are not meant to work all the time. We must rest, pour ourselves into hobbies, and connect with family members and friends to fully experience life.

While the wildfire metaphor serves many purposes, it is certainly not one-size-fits-all, and it may not be relevant for every situation. My hope is that you have seen its value and understand how to apply it to your own life and special circumstances.

CHAPTER 5

Burnout Prevention

IF YOU TAKE NOTHING ELSE from this book, I hope you see that burnout recovery is a long process. It takes time. One vacation is not going to "fix" burnout. This book is intended to serve as a long-term road map. It will take twenty to thirty years for the Hermit's Peak / Calf Canyon fire scar near my home to truly dissolve back into the wilderness. Recovering from burnout takes time—time measured in years, not months. Be gentle with yourself and celebrate all the small wins that occur. In the healing process, any progress is a good thing.

Early Awareness of Stress Can Prevent Burnout

As I write this, it's the annual fire season in New Mexico. The air and land are dry, the wind is high, the temperatures are warm. The slightest spark falling on the winter-dried plants will ignite a new fire, and with gusting winds over fifty miles per hour, any fire can become a wildfire. Wildfire is always a risk and always a reality here, and it is something that we must collectively work to prevent. Each April, I refresh my evacuation kits, review the yard work that needs to be done to protect my house, and avoid any activity that might cause a spark. This kind of routine maintenance and care is equally important for preventing future burnout.

We know, when it's a busy time of year or a crunch time with multiple projects and deadlines, that "fire season" may be upon us. While burnout isn't a foregone conclusion or even imminent, the risk factors are all there for a fire to ignite and spread. During times of temporary stress, it is important that we do the preventive self-care necessary to ensure that it does not escalate into chronic stress or another round of burnout. There are several recovery tools outlined in the earlier chapters of this book that are useful to have at hand when "fire season" begins in your life.

Daily Self-Care Tools and the PERMA+H Model

Each spring, I assess the fire risk around my house in concentric circles. Ten feet from the house, I have to cut down and remove long grass and volunteer trees. Thirty feet from the house, I need to trim back shrubs and trees. Fifty feet from the house, I need to be sure my trees are healthy and that their canopies are not at risk of burning. I need to be sure firefighters can find my house, that their trucks can get in and out of my driveway safely, and that water is available if they must fight a fire. Having this regular mental checklist is a way of keeping my home safe and healthy, regardless of whether any fires have started nearby or not. This section is about those daily and regular habits we all need to cultivate to ensure that we are safe from the fires of burnout and resilient in the event of a flare of stress.

Martin Seligman, the cofounder of positive psychology, developed a model that helps people achieve wellness and thrive (rather than just reduce symptoms).[1] Many of the exercises outlined in this book are based upon this model, which is known by the acronym PERMA+H. This stands for:

P – Positive thinking

E – Engagement

R – Relationships

M – Meaning

A – Achievement

H – Health

The "H" wasn't originally part of the model; it was added in 2020 after Seligman and his team were made more clearly aware of the role health and healthy habits can have in our thriving.

Positive Thinking

One does not have to be Pollyanna or naïve to think positively. The brain is constantly trying to solve our problems. Most of the time, it is looking for ways to keep us safe, to prevent disaster, and so on. This form of problem-solving often feels like worry and anxiety, and it can lead to stress spirals; if you are actively looking for things to worry about, you will find plenty of them! However, we can stop this cycle by asking our brains to look, instead, for positive things: lucky coincidences, happy things, beautiful things. If we intentionally point out positive things to our brain, it will begin to learn to look for positive events. The "Three Good Things" exercise (page 30) is one way to trick your brain into looking for the good things each day.

A positive thinker sees bad things that happen as *temporary* and as being the result of a one-time event. They see good things that happen as *frequent* and as resulting from who they are and how they navigate the world. Adopting this thought pattern is often a goal of therapy. Depression and addiction are often exacerbated by—or even caused by—the opposite thought patterns, which see our negative life events as being due to who we are as people and as a regularly occurring circumstance. We don't have to delve into this further here, but it's important to know that getting into the habit of listing three good things that happen every day *does* work. Repeated studies show that this one tactic changes our outlook more powerfully than any other.

Engagement

Engagement is more commonly referred to as *flow state*. Getting to experience a sense of "flow" every day is one of the best ways to avoid burnout. The book *Flow: The Psychology of Optimal Experience* by Mihaly Csikszentmihalyi gets into the science behind it, but the idea is that you're engaged in something that's just difficult enough to be challenging, but not so difficult as to be overwhelming or discouraging.[2] Flow might be experienced while doing hobbies or while at work; whenever it seems like time is standing still, that's flow. The emotional experience of a flow state is often a neutral one, because all the emotional and mental energy is being funneled into the activity itself, but entering a state of flow each day leaves us with a sense of accomplishment and emotional well-being. The feeling of time standing still and having a single point of focus on an activity is deeply satisfying and healing to our minds and hearts.

As discussed in chapter 2, flow states occur when we are doing something we're relatively good at, but which is still novel and challenging. Often, we find these states in sporting activity, creative acts, hobbies, or work. It's a little silly to say it, but I achieve some of my best flow states when I'm creating presentation decks. It may sound unrealistic to recommend entering a flow state daily. However, the more you can build into your life those activities that offer the flow state to you, the more resilient you will be against future burnout.

Relationships

Later in this chapter, I will be writing about "graduating" from your support team, but there's a reason why I recommended recruiting your team members very early in the burnout-recovery process. Having supportive, meaningful connections with other people is a vital part of being a happy, healthy human being. We have evolved into being very social animals, and we require community and connection to survive.

As you've navigated this process, it's very likely that you've come to realize that you cannot easily or reasonably meet all of your social needs with one single relationship. When one person plays too many roles, it can shatter the relationship you have with them. It's important to maintain contact with many of the important people in your life.

Social media pretends to offer meaningful connection with the people in our lives, and while it sometimes truly can spark that kind of emotional connection, it's very rare. Clicking "like" on a friend's social-media post is not the same as maintaining a meaningful connection. Close friendships and support systems share trust, respect, vulnerability, and honesty. We are often not wholly honest or vulnerable on our own social-media posts.

Still, some dedicated online communities provide valuable ways to connect with other people. Usually these spaces are not open to our friends and family members, and we are able to be a little more vulnerable in an anonymous, but supportive, area of the internet.

I live alone, in the middle of nowhere, and most of my friends are scattered all over the country. I use weekly scheduled phone calls, regular text exchanges, and Zoom calls with groups or individuals to stay in contact with my support community. Naturally, if and when I'm able to meet up with them in person, I do so. However, the most important thing is to stay in touch and create genuine connection with the people in our lives. This requires effort and time, but it is invaluable.

Meaning

In chapter 2, I wrote about ensuring that our work activities have *meaning*: that they align with and reflect our deep inner values and beliefs. This is another way of building and maintaining a healthy inner landscape. It also makes the crunch times a little easier to tolerate.

It's unrealistic to think that every job or career in the world is a meaningful one. What is possible is to find meaning in *why* you are working to begin with. Do you have a family or a pet you are providing for? Are you working simply for the ability to pay rent and afford to eat healthy food? Is that sense of safety, security, and self-reliance not meaningful? I think it is. The journaling exercises outlined in chapter 2 are aimed at helping us remember those deeper meanings that fuel what we do.

As we all explore what's next in our professional lives, finding meaningful work that is aligned with our inner values and dreams is an ongoing challenge.

Achievement

There is a moment after completing a job when we get to mark a task as done and just bask for a few seconds in the glow of accomplishment. The little boost in our self-confidence and the sense of efficacy that we get from this is part of an overall state of well-being.

In chapter 2, I recommended completing a strengths assessment and doing something we're good at every single day. This is tied to the "Achievement" part of the PERMA+H model. Doing things we're good at, and completing them, helps us to better feel which areas of our lives we have influence and control over and which areas we do not.

I find that this lens is also useful when I'm bumping into frustration at work. If I am not feeling a sense of accomplishment or achievement, I need to evaluate the kind of work I'm doing and whether it enables me to use my strengths. If we're not being set up for success, we need to talk with our manager or supervisor. When we're not able to use our strengths at work, it's frustrating for everyone. It's also an easy way to feel helpless and burned out. Having a sense of doing your job well can help ensure that your job is working for you.

Health

The "H" at the end of the PERMA acronym was added in 2020, after the COVID-19 pandemic had begun. Many people realized that taking steps to support and maintain our physical health was vital to psycho-logical thriving and a sense of well-being. The basics of body mainte-nance, such as sleep and nutritious food, are important for creating a sustainable, resilient self-care routine. Studies on the stress-managing and stress-reducing effects of exercise are innumerable; as few as twenty minutes spent walking each day can improve resilience,[3] a sense of well-being,[4] and self-regulation.[5]

I would like to suggest, as well, that proper physical self-care includes having healthy boundaries and the ability to say "no." When by myself and left to my own devices, I'm able to make relatively healthy choices around diet, exercise, sleep, and physical self-care. These choices tend to get derailed when there are other people in the mix. I sometimes have to say "no" to social outings if I still have to work out that day, or I need to stand firm in my choice to not drink alcohol at a social gathering. Of course, healthy living is all about balance, so an occasional late night or missed workout isn't catastrophic. However, this is where asserting those boundaries comes in, to ensure that it's a one-time event and not a new normal.

Using the Metaphor as a Long-Term Road Map

Just as each spring comes with the threat of new fires, it's always possible that you will catch yourself burning out again in the future. Remember, landscapes that have been burned are among the most at risk of future fires. Likewise, if your personality, work ethic, and career already make you prone to burnout, you are almost always at risk of burning out again.

The key here is to catch it early, before it spreads. Notice your anger and let yourself feel and process it when boundaries are violated. Assert those boundaries and enforce them to contain the fire early. Take steps to ramp up your stress-mitigating self-care during times when burnout threatens. The wildfire metaphor remains available for you to revisit and determine, again, where you are in the cycle.

It's not unusual for each of us to cycle into and out of burnout multiple times, especially if we are staying at the same workplace or on the same career path. Often, a more drastic career change becomes necessary after repeated burnout cycles. My hope is that the tools in this book will help you determine when that is the case for you. Using the emotions you're feeling to determine where you are now in the burnout cycle, you can revisit the exercises and activities for that section in the book.

Graduating from Your Support Team and Supporting Them in Return

At some point, you will feel like you have moved beyond recovery and into long-term burnout prevention. As mentioned above regarding the importance of community and social support, it's vital that we acknowledge the support team that has helped us through this journey.

Graduating from a support team does not have to be official or formal. Some shifts may simply feel natural over time. For example, you might find yourself dropping back from weekly therapy sessions to biweekly or even monthly. However, you may find it a worthwhile ritual to select and offer each one of the members of your support team a small card or thank-you gift, acknowledging their role in your burnout recovery. A ritual of this sort can signal to your unconscious that you have crossed a threshold and are embarking on a new journey.

One of the first signs that it's time to graduate from your support team is noticing that you have stopped being the one who is supported and instead are lending a hand to them. Because you've shared your journey, with varying degrees of trust and vulnerability, with these people in your life, it's very likely that they will see you as someone they can similarly trust. "Paying it forward" is a beautiful way to help others stop the burnout cycle and recover their inner peace.

You may not ever fully realize the ripple effects that your healing journey has on the people around you. I like to imagine each of us as rocks tossed into a pond. If we're the rock, steadily seeing our progress as we dive to the bottom of the pond, the sunlight growing dimmer and more filtered before we land in a puff of silt, we do not realize the effect of our movement on the surface of the pond. We don't know how many ripples spread out from us, how big of a splash was created, or how long the ripples took to dissipate back to stillness.

Every now and then, someone will let us know that we created a ripple in their lives. Your healing journey might inspire your coworker to undertake their own. It may inspire your spouse to revisit a dusty hobby hidden on a closet shelf. The members of your support team are the likeliest people to be positively inspired and motivated by your self-care. Offering the same support back to them, as they embark on their own healing processes, is one of the greatest ways you can repay them.

Resources

Recommended Further Reading

Authentic Happiness: Using the New Positive Psychology to Realize Your Potential for Lasting Fulfillment by Martin E. P. Seligman

Burnout: The Secret to Unlocking the Stress Cycle by Emily Nagoski and Amelia Nagoski

Decolonizing Therapy: Oppression, Historical Trauma, and Politicizing Your Practice by Jennifer Mullan

Ecopsychology: Restoring the Earth, Healing the Mind by Theodore Roszak, Mary E. Gomes, and Allen D. Kanner

Ecotherapy: Healing with Nature in Mind by Linda Buzzell and Craig Chalquist

Flourish: A Visionary New Understanding of Happiness and Well-Being by Martin E. P. Seligman

Flow: The Psychology of Optimal Experience by Mihaly Csikszentmihalyi

Heal Your Relationship with Money: Understand Your Money "Why," Let Go of Your Past Financial Dysfunction, and Make Peace with Your Money Life in Just 28 Days by Kara Stevens

The Hope Circuit: A Psychologist's Journey from Helplessness to Optimism by Martin E. P. Seligman

Living with Wildfires: Prevention, Preparation, and Recovery by Janet C. Arrowood

My Grandmother's Hands: Racialized Trauma and the Pathway to Mending Our Hearts and Bodies by Resmaa Menakem

The Racial Healing Handbook: Practical Activities to Help You Challenge Privilege, Confront Systemic Racism, and Engage in Collective Healing by Anneliese A. Singh

Self-Care for Black Men: 100 Ways to Heal and Liberate by Jor-El Caraballo

The Unapologetic Guide to Black Mental Health: Navigate an Unequal System, Learn Tools for Emotional Wellness, and Get the Help You Deserve by Rheeda Walker

Websites and Helplines

Suicide and Crisis Centers

988 SUICIDE AND CRISIS LIFELINE

Call or text 988 (available in English and Spanish)

Chat at www.988lifeline.org

CRISIS TEXT LINE (CTL)

Text HOME to 741741

SUBSTANCE ABUSE AND MENTAL HEALTH SERVICES ADMINISTRATION (SAMHSA)

National helpline: 1-800-662-HELP

Racial Trauma and Stress

BLACK EMOTIONAL AND MENTAL HEALTH COLLECTIVE (BEAM)

https://beam.community

LGBTQIA+ Stress and Support

TRANS LIFELINE

Call or text 877-565-8860

THE TREVOR PROJECT

www.thetrevorproject.org

Call 1-866-488-7386 or text "START" to 678-678

Climate Anxiety Resources

DISASTER DISTRESS HELPLINE

Call or text 1-800-985-5990

ALL WE CAN SAVE PROJECT

www.allwecansave.earth/emotions

MENTAL HEALTH AND CLIMATE CHANGE ALLIANCE (MHCCA)

https://mhcca.ca

Notes

Foreword

1 Clayton et al., *Mental Health and Our Changing Climate*.

Introduction

1 Fisher, "Workplace Burnout Survey."

2 World Health Organization, "Burn-Out an 'Occupational Phenomenon.'"

3 Freud, *General Psychological Theory*, 116–150. Freud's theory of the unconscious evolved through his work on dreams and with repressed memories in patients diagnosed with hysteria. His first major essay on the topic was "The Unconscious," in 1915, which is included in *General Psychological Theory: Papers on Metapsychology*, the 1963 English-language text edited by Philip Rieff.

4 Jung, *The Essential Jung*, 66–68, from "On the Psychology of the Unconscious." Like Freud, Jung continued to develop his theories about the unconscious and the collective unconscious throughout his life.

5 Palmer, "Can Ecopsychology Research Inform Coaching and Positive Psychology Practice?"

6 Kalsched, *The Inner World of Trauma*, 1.

7 Kalsched, *The Inner World of Trauma*, 23.

Chapter 1: The Metaphor and Where You Are Within the Burnout Cycle

1 Gerringer, "Joseph Campbell's Four Functions of Myth." See also Campbell, *The Hero With A Thousand Faces*, 28–31.

2 Campbell and Moyers, *The Power of Myth*, 39.

3 Campbell and Moyers, *The Power of Myth*, 39.

4 As quoted in Gerringer, "Joseph Campbell's Four Functions of Myth."

5 Seligman, *Flourish*, 12.

Chapter 2: Applying the Wildfire Metaphor to Professional Burnout

1 Franco, "Employee Assistance Statistics and Utilization Rates."

2 Seligman et al., Positive Psychology Progress."

3 Kroenke et al., "The PHQ-9."

4 The Labyrinth Locator is an excellent tool to help find labyrinths close to you: https://labyrinthlocator.org.

5 Jeffrey, "The Ultimate List of Core Values"; Covey, "Build Your Mission Statement."

6 Kemp, "Ikigai Misunderstood and the Origin of the Ikigai Venn Diagram."

7 More information is available about these tests at https://high5test.com, www.viacharacter.org, and https://strengthsbasedresilience.com.

Chapter 3: Applying the Wildfire Metaphor to Neurodivergent Burnout

1 CPTSD is a form of post-traumatic stress that is caused by repeated stressors rather than a single, large traumatic event (as in classic PTSD).

2 Six Seconds, "Plutchik's Wheel of Emotions."

3 Kapp et al., "'People Should Be Allowed to Do What They Like.'"

4 Children's Hospital of Philadelphia Research Institute, "Stimming."

5 ASMR stands for "Autonomous Sensory Motor Response" and refers to the relaxing tingly sensations that some people experience when they listen to certain sounds or see certain visual triggers. There are a wide variety of "ASMRtists" on YouTube who offer a huge array of triggers for viewers to experiment with.

Chapter 4: When It's Not Just Burnout

1 For more about poverty and burnout, see De Schutter, 2024.

2 Kalsched, *The Inner World of Trauma*, 23.

3 Cohen, "The Way out of Burnout."

Chapter 5: Burnout Prevention

1 Seligman, *Flourish*.

2 Csikszentmihalyi, *Flow*.

3 Childs and De Wit, "Regular Exercise Is Associated with Emotional Resilience to Acute Stress in Healthy Adults."

4 Mahindru et al., "Role of Physical Activity on Mental Health and Well-Being."

5 Bahri, et al., "The Relationship between Walking and Depression, Anxiety, and Stress among a Sample from Jazan, Saudi Arabia."

Bibliography

Arrowood, Janet C. *Living with Wildfires: Prevention, Preparation, and Recovery.* Bradford Publishing Company, 2003.

Bahri, Ahmed A., Hasan A. Korairi, Ibrahim M. Gosadi, Faisal A. Othathi, Mohammed O. Shami, and Mohammad A. Jareebi. "The Relationship between Walking and Depression, Anxiety, and Stress among a Sample from Jazan, Saudi Arabia: A Cross-Sectional Investigation." *Medicine* 101, no. 38 (2022), https://doi.org/10.1097/MD.0000000000030718.

Buzzell, Linda, and Craig Chalquist. *Ecotherapy: Healing with Nature in Mind.* Sierra Club Books, 2009.

Campbell, Joseph, and Bill D. Moyers. *The Power of Myth.* Doubleday, 1988.

Campbell, Joseph. *The Hero With A Thousand Faces.* New World Library, 2008.

Caraballo, Jor-El. *Self-Care for Black Men: 100 Ways to Heal and Liberate.* Adams Media, 2023.

Children's Hospital of Philadelphia Research Institute. "Stimming: What Is It and Does It Matter?" Updated May 29, 2020. https://www.research.chop .edu/car-autism-roadmap/stimming-what-is-it-and-does-it-matter.

Childs, Emma, and Harriet de Wit. "Regular Exercise Is Associated with Emotional Resilience to Acute Stress in Healthy Adults." *Frontiers in Physiology* 5, no. 161 (2014), https://doi.org/10.3389/fphys.2014.00161.

Clayton, Susan, Christie Manning, Kirra Krygsman, and Meighen Speiser. *Mental Health and Our Changing Climate: Impacts, Implications, and Guidance* (American Psychological Association, 2017), https://www.apa.org/ news/press/releases/2017/03/mental-health-climate.pdf.

Cohen, Josh, "The Way Out of Burnout," *The Economist* (1843 magazine), July 28, 2016, https://www.economist.com/1843/2016/07/28/the-way-out -of-burnout.

Covey, Stephen R. n.d. "Build Your Mission Statement." FranklinCovey. Accessed June 12, 2025. https://msb.franklincovey.com.

Csikszentmihalyi, Mihaly. *Flow: The Psychology of Optimal Experience.* Harper Perennial, 1991.

De Schutter, Olivier. "The Burnout Economy: Poverty and Mental Health." Report of the Special Rapporteur on extreme poverty and human rights. United Nations General Assembly, July 16, 2024. https://docs.un.org /en/A/79/162.

Fisher, Jen. n.d. "Workplace Burnout Survey: Burnout without Borders." Deloitte United States. Accessed June 12, 2025. https://www2.deloitte .com/us/en/pages/about-deloitte/articles/burnout-survey.html.

Franco, Daniela D. "Employee Assistance Programs Statistics and Utilization Rates," Meditopia for Work. Updated June 11, 2025. https://meditopia .com/en/forwork/articles/eap-statistics-and-utilization-rates.

Freud, Sigmund. *General Psychological Theory: Papers on Metapsychology.* Edited by Philip Rieff. Collier Books, 1963.

Gerringer, Stephen. n.d. "Joseph Campbell's Four Functions of Myth." Joseph Campbell Foundation. Accessed June 12, 2025. https://www.jcf.org/learn /joseph-campbell-four-functions-of-myth.

Jeffrey, Scott. "The Ultimate List of Core Values (Over 230)." CEOsage. Updated October 1, 2024. https://scottjeffrey.com/core-values-list.

Jung, C. G. *The Essential Jung.* Edited by Anthony Storr. Princeton University Press, 2013.

Kalsched, Donald. *The Inner World of Trauma.* Routledge, 2008.

Kapp, Steven K., Robyn Steward, Laura Crane, Daisy Elliott, Chris Elphick, Elizabeth Pellicano, and Ginny Russell. "'People Should Be Allowed to Do What They Like': Autistic Adults' Views and Experiences of Stimming." *Autism* 23, no. 7 (2019): 1782–92. https://doi.org/10.1177/1362361319829628.

Kemp, Nicholas. "Ikigai Misunderstood and the Origin of the Ikigai Venn Diagram." Ikigai Tribe, July 23, 2019. https://ikigaitribe.com/ikigai/ikigai -misunderstood.

Kroenke, Kurt, Robert L. Spitzer, and Janet B. Williams. "The PHQ-9: Validity of A Brief Depression Severity Measure." *Journal of General Internal Medicine* 16 (2001): 606–13. https://doi.org/10.1046/j.1525-1497.2001.016009606.x.

Mahindru, Aditya, Pradeep Patil, and Varun Agrawal. "Role of Physical Activity on Mental Health and Well-Being: A Review." *Cureus* 15, no. 1 (2023). https://doi.org/10.7759/cureus.33475.

Maté, Gabor. *When the Body Says No: Exploring the Stress-Disease Connection.* Turner Publishing, 2011.

Menakem, Resmaa. *My Grandmother's Hands: Racialized Trauma and the Pathway to Mending Our Hearts and Bodies.* Central Recovery Press, 2021.

Mullan, Jennifer. *Decolonizing Therapy: Oppression, Historical Trauma, and Politicizing Your Practice.* W. W. Norton, 2023.

Nagoski, Emily, and Amelia Nagoski. *Burnout: The Secret to Unlocking the Stress Cycle.* Ballantine Books, 2020.

Palmer, S. "Can Ecopsychology Research Inform Coaching and Positive Psychology Practice?" *Coaching Psychology International* 8, no. 1 (2015): 11–15.

Roszak, Theodore, Mary E. Gomes, and Allen D. Kanner. *Ecopsychology: Restoring the Earth, Healing the Mind.* Sierra Club Books, 1997.

Seligman, Martin E. P. *Authentic Happiness: Using the New Positive Psychology to Realize Your Potential for Lasting Fulfillment.* Atria, 2013.

Seligman, Martin E. P. *Flourish: A Visionary New Understanding of Happiness and Well-Being.* Atria, 2013.

Seligman, Martin E. P. *The Hope Circuit: A Psychologist's Journey from Helplessness to Optimism.* PublicAffairs, 2018.

Seligman, Martin E., Tracy A. Steen, Nansook Park, and Christopher Peterson. "Positive Psychology Progress: Empirical Validation of Interventions." *American Psychologist* 60, no. 5 (July 2005): 410–21. https://doi.org/10.1037/0003-066x.60.5.410.

Singh, Anneliese A. *The Racial Healing Handbook: Practical Activities to Help You Challenge Privilege, Confront Systemic Racism, and Engage in Collective Healing.* New Harbinger Publications, 2019.

Six Seconds. n.d. "Plutchik's Wheel of Emotions: Exploring the Feelings Wheel and How to Use It." Accessed June 12, 2025, https://www.6seconds.org/2022/03/13/plutchik-wheel-emotions.

Stevens, Kara. *Heal Your Relationship with Money: Understanding Your Money "Why," Let Go of Your Past Financial Dysfunction, and Make Peace with Your Money Life in Just 28 Days.* Frugal Feminista, 2019.

van der Kolk, Bessel. *The Body Keeps the Score: Brain, Mind, and Body in the Healing of Trauma.* Viking, 2014.

Walker, Rheeda. *The Unapologetic Guide to Black Mental Health: Navigate an Unequal System, Learn Tools for Emotional Wellness, and Get the Help You Deserve.* New Harbinger Publications, 2021.

World Health Organization. n.d. "Burn-Out an 'Occupational Phenomenon.'" Accessed June 12, 2025. https://www.who.int/standards/classifications /frequently-asked-questions/burn-out-an-occupational-phenomenon.

Index

Acknowledgments

In this book, I recommend assembling a support team of people who can help with the process of escaping from the burnout cycle and achieving long-term recovery. I am eternally grateful for the members of my own support team who have come and gone over the last decade. The current team includes Joshua Brown, Sara Butler, Kim Richardson, Kara Suzelis, John Adams, Dr. Amy Slonaker, Dr. Carol Myers, Dr. Jacqueline Wright, and Dr. Alexa Schriempf. Previous support team members include Brett Anderson, Tom Roseberry, Michelle Chen, Kenneth Hamner, and many, many more.

This book would not be possible without the amazing team at North Atlantic Books. Gillian Hamel, Jasmine Respess, Janelle Ludowise, Erin Wiegand, and the many others who contributed to and worked on this book in the past year and have added to it greatly. Thank you all for understanding the book's goal and vision and helping me to bring it to fruition.

I also want to thank Loraine Van Tuyl and Claudia Castillo Holley, whose Taos retreat in 2023 helped me to get in touch with my own inner Fire and learn to use it wisely. I'd like to thank Margaret Brown for guiding me through the process of naming my emotions over twenty years ago.

I'm grateful for books and authors that have inspired me in the creation of this work, as well as some of the exercises I've included. These books include *The Artist's Way* by Julia Cameron, *The Inner World of Trauma* by Donald Kalsched, and Dr. Martin Seligman's entire body of work. I owe a debt of gratitude to Dr. Craig Chalquist and other pioneers in the field of ecopsychology.

Finally, I would like to extend my deepest appreciation to ecopsychologist Linda Buzzell for offering a foreword for this book.

About the Author

Alicia K. Anderson has a PhD in mythological studies with an emphasis in depth psychology, from Pacifica Graduate Institute. Her dissertation on the Storyteller archetype explores the responsibilities of storytellers. Her areas of interest include career pivots and transitions; trauma; burnout; fairy tales (particularly fairy tale retellings); mythology retellings; and archetypal symbols such as the tarot and unicorns. She has scholarly chapters forthcoming in two volumes by Vernon Press and is currently editing a collection of essays called *Essays on Advanced Unicorn Theory,* which will be published by McFarland in 2026. Anderson has presented at the American Folklore Society annual meeting, the London Arts-Based Research Center conference "The Art of Storytelling: Archetypes in Focus," the Southwest Popular/American Culture Association conference, and at the Progressive Connexions conference "Trauma, Shame, and Testimony." She offers workshops, 1:1 coaching, and on-demand online courses on achieving lasting burnout recovery.

The author wishes to extend a special thanks to her Patreon members John, Christine, Vince, Renée, Alicia, Nancy, Victoria, Ame, Gilena, and Lex.

About North Atlantic Books

North Atlantic Books (NAB) is an independent, nonprofit publisher committed to a bold exploration of the relationships between mind, body, spirit, and nature. Founded in 1974, NAB aims to nurture a holistic view of the arts, sciences, humanities, and healing. To make a donation or to learn more about our books, authors, events, and newsletter, please visit www.northatlanticbooks.com.